www.wadsworth.com

wadsworth.com is the World Wide Web site for Wadsworth and is your direct source to dozens of online resources.

At *wadsworth.com* you can find out about supplements, demonstration software, and student resources. You can also send email to many of our authors and preview new publications and exciting new technologies.

wadsworth.com
Changing the way the world learns®

Piano for Pleasure

A Basic Course for Adults

Fourth Edition

Martha Hilley
The University of Texas at Austin

Lynn Freeman Olson

SCHIRMER
THOMSON LEARNING

Australia • Canada • Mexico • Singapore • Spain
United Kingdom • United States

SCHIRMER
™
THOMSON LEARNING

Editorial Director for the Humanities: Clark G. Baxter
Assistant Editor: Jennifer Ellis
Editorial Assistant: Jonathan Katz
Executive Marketing Manager: Diane McOscar
Marketing Assistant: Kasia Zagorski
Project Manager: Dianne Jensis Toop
Print/Media Buyer: Karen Hunt
Permissions Editor: Joohee Lee
Production Service: A-R Editions, Inc.

Copy Editor: A-R Editions, Inc.
Cover Designer: Andrew Ogus
Cover Image: Paul Klee (1879–1940) *Fire by Moonlight*, 1933.
  © Giraudon/Art Resource, NY
Cover Printer: Malloy Lithographing, Inc
Compositor: A-R Editions, Inc.
Printer: Malloy Lithographing, Inc.

For more information about our products, contact us:
Thomson Learning Academic Resource Center
1-800-423-0563
http://www.wadsworth.com

International Headquarters
Thomson Learning
International Division
290 Harbor Drive, 2nd Floor
Stamford, CT 06902-7477
USA

UK/Europe/Middle East/South Africa
Thomson Learning
Berkshire House
168-173 High Holborn
London WC1V 7AA
United Kingdom

Asia
Thomson Learning
60 Albert Street, #15-01
Albert Complex
Singapore 189969

Canada
Nelson Thomson Learning
1120 Birchmount Road
Toronto, Ontario M1K 5G4
Canada

Wadsworth/Thomson Learning
10 Davis Drive
Belmont, CA 94002-3098
USA

ISBN 0-534-51962-8

Dedication

To the people in our little hometown of Spur, Texas, she is L. G.; to so many "kids" who now have kids of their own she is Mrs. Nay, the music teacher who planted a love for music in their hearts; to so many of my students and graduate assistants she is "Mama"; to my friends and her friends and large majority of the music industry, she is "Miz Lillian"; to me, she is my rock, my best friend and my precious mother. This is the year of her "elegant 80th". May I some day approach this age with the same style, grace, wit and zest for living as she has.

You are a joy to all who cross your path, sweet one. Thank you for always being there.

Contents

Listening/Dynamics/Black Keys

Simple Note Values/Key Names/Black-Key Groups

3. Meter Signatures/Rests/Line and Space Notes/Steps and Skips/Seconds and Thirds

4. Recap

5. Treble and Bass/Grand Staff/Fourths and Fifths/Half Steps and Whole Steps/Sharps and Flats

6. Dotted Rhythms/Phrases

7. Upbeats/Major Pentascales

Recap

Extensions/Triads/Ledger Lines

10. Syncopation/Sixths, Sevenths, Eighths/Major Scales Key Signatures

11. Scale Fingering/Primary Chords/Harmonizing/ Transposing

12. Recap

3. Chord Inversions/Guitar Symbols

14. Sixteenth Notes/Interval Quality/Dominant Sevenths

15. Compound Meter/Key Triads

16. Recap

17. Triplets/Primary Chords in Minor

18. Holiday Repertoire

19. Supplementary Repertoire

Preface

Welcome back, once again!

We are a lucky lot—music is still a pleasure, and many people continue to satisfy the need for that pleasure with the keyboard. Music is often quite personal. You may not feel immediately at home with every piece or activity in this book. However, variety is the spice of life, and so it is with music. You should plan to reach out and try, but know that some will simply not be "yours" at once.

Music is sound, not notes, signs, or terms. We have kept the original format and begin again with **Listening**. What you learn with your ears actively involved will always be with you. An audio CD and MIDI disks are available with each adoption. Your teacher may allow you to copy any examples you wish. These sound sources are an integral part of this publication and should be used whenever possible.

All of the activities have the purpose of increasing your knowledge and skill (and thus your pleasure), so dig in—and be patient with yourself. The moment you participate, you are beginning to learn.

Rhythm is essential. The tapping exercises can be performed on any surface—no need to wait for a piano! Always relax into a steady beat.

Technique is simply the *way* you achieve sounds. "Tabletop" exercises do not require a piano, so launch into them whenever and wherever you can.

Theory is the whys and the wherefores as well as the terminology—but is still brought to the piano.

Reading principles and drills provide a way for you to translate written symbols into sound. Regular practice will allow you to possess this skill.

Improvising brings music to life and helps make its expression most personal; jump in and try: there is no wrong solution to an improvisation assignment.

Performance is a natural part of music. In a very real sense, music cannot live until it is performed. Enjoy playing at every step along the way, at each level you reach.

Develop the following qualities as you move through these materials with your teacher:

> **Curiosity**—ask "why" and "how"
> **Confidence**—jump in, play the piano, and keep going no matter what!
> **Patience**—take the time to let your ears, mind, and muscles learn (they will!)
> **Industry**—In general, you cannot *will* these skills into being; you must devote some time for workouts on a regular basis.

The bottom line is always enjoyment—music for the lifelong values of personal achievement, aesthetic awareness, emotional expression, and social interaction.

It's a pleasure to welcome you to the world of music at the piano.

Acknowledgments

Piano for Pleasure has been just that—a pleasure—from the very day of the birth of the idea. For those of you who knew Lynn Freeman Olson, you know that he believed in the joy and wonder that comes from music and spent his life sharing that belief with all who would listen.

Thanks must continue to those who gave so freely of their talent to the initial publication through the audio cassette; **pianists:** Esther Chung, Denise Chupp Mullins, Steve Havens, William Chapman Nyaho, Greg Partain, Jay Surdell, and William Wellborn and a special thought to the memory of Chuck Vinson; **The Haydon Jazz Quartet:** Geoff Haydon, Barry McVinney, William McKay, and Shaun Smith; **strings:** Cathy Haines, Elliott Cheney, Laurie Stevens, and Kerri Lay; **recording engineers:** Bob Roberts and Ray Fishel; a special thought to the memory of **producer, director, and narrator:** Dr. Merrill Staton. The cassette is now housed on a CD and will be shipped with each book.

At the college level *Piano for Pleasure* is used primarily by "non-music majors"—those future engineers, business tycoons, chemist and computer gurus who either finally have the chance to fulfill a lifelong dream of learning to play the piano or who say "I wish my Mother hadn't let me quit." This makes this clientele a very special bunch. They want to learn—everything is a "wonder" to them and they revel in their slightest accomplishments. I want to acknowledge this very special dose of passion and joy they bring to the classroom. Don't ever lose it!

There aren't enouth ways to say thank you to Clark and Abigail Baxter for the bottomless barrel of support, to Bonnie Balke (A-R Editions), I have just gotten to know you and already it has been a pleasure. To Pam Suwinsky (Wadsworth Group), thank you for your patience and understanding. And as always, to Lynn and all the memories I have of our work together I am forever grateful.

Martha Hilley

Piano for Pleasure

A Basic Course for Adults

Fourth Edition

2

1.

Listening/Dynamics/Black Keys

LISTENING

Listen to the recorded examples; determine the "feel" of each. Is there a "feel" for 2s; a "feel" for 3s?

RHYTHM

1. Listen to the recorded examples. Some are "in 2," some "in 3." Determine the feel and tap strong pulses.

   Example:

   "in 2":   TAP (*off*) TAP (*off*)

   "in 3":   TAP __ __ TAP __ __

2. Place the CD on 1-2. Play with the recorded examples, this time playing strong pulses with your left hand as you fill in the other pulses with your right hand. Use single black keys in each hand.

   Example:

   "in 2":   PLAY   play   PLAY   play   PLAY   *etc.*
               LH   rh   LH   rh   LH

   "in 3":   PLAY   play   play   PLAY   play   play   *etc.*
               LH   rh   rh   LH   rh   rh

This is an improvisation, so feel free to explore the full range of the keyboard on any black keys.

TECHNIQUE

In keyboard study, fingers are numbered as follows.

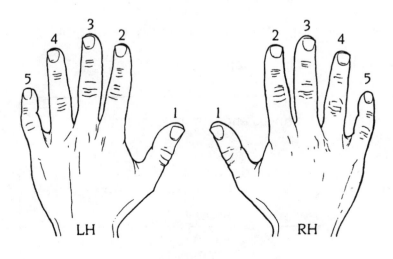

Let your arms hang at your sides. Notice how the fingers are slightly curved at the middle joint. This [is] a natural, unforced, relaxed hand position. Place both hands on a flat surface in front of you. Maint[ain] the natural shape of your hand. Notice the slightly "rounded" condition of your fingers and overall hand shape; this is the most natural and best position for your hands in playing the piano.

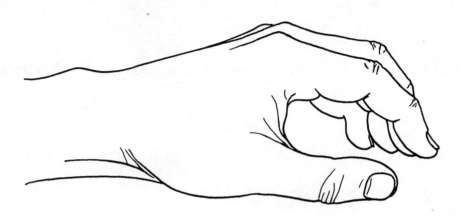

1-3

Follow the directions on the CD as you are asked to tap corresponding fingers together. If using the disk background, follow your teacher's directions.

THEORY

Dynamics are very important elements in any music.

1-4

1. Perform the following exercises with the dynamic level indicated as the CD or MIDI disk provides musical background.

LOUD:	Tap	Clap	Tap	Clap	*etc.*		
SOFT:	Tap	Clap	Clap	Tap	Clap	Clap	*etc.*
LOUD:	Tap	Clap	Clap	Clap			
	Tap	Clap	Clap	Clap	*etc.*		

2. Repeat the following pattern eight times starting softly, getting louder, and ending softly.

Tap   Clap   Clap   Clap

Dynamics   Degrees of loudness and softness; intensity
Forte   Loud (f)
Piano   Soft (p)
Crescendo   To get gradually louder (cresc., or $<$)
Decrescendo   To get gradually softer (decresc., or $>$)

READING

1-5

Tabletop reading. With both hands on a flat surface, play the following exercises with the CD or MIDI disk background (dash means "hold").

Exercise 1

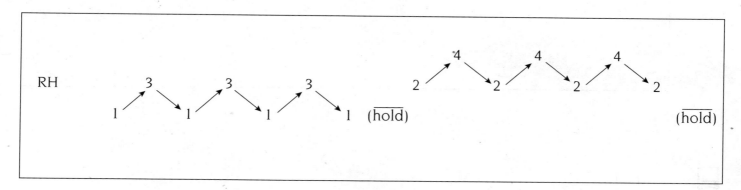

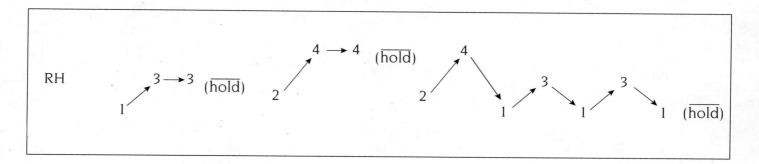

Exercise 2

Exercise 3

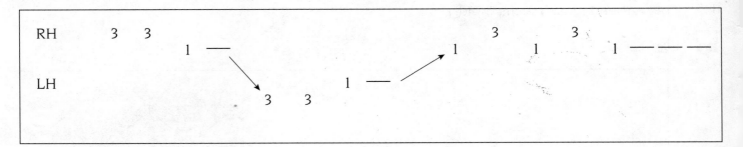

Exercise 4

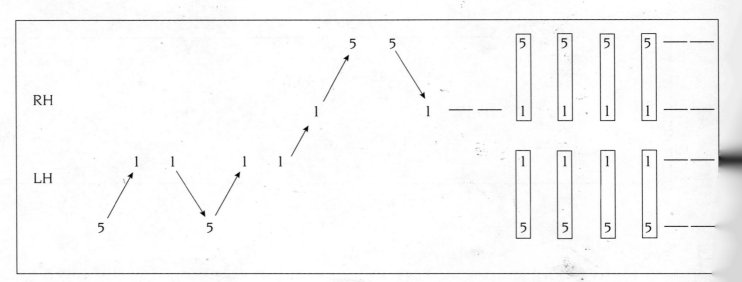

Exercise 5

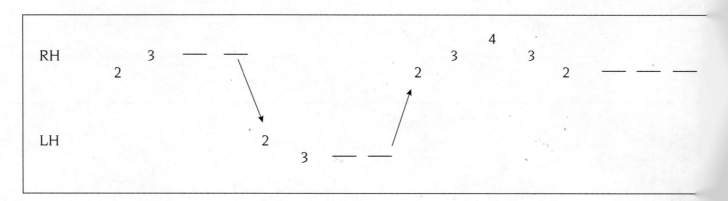

Exercise 6

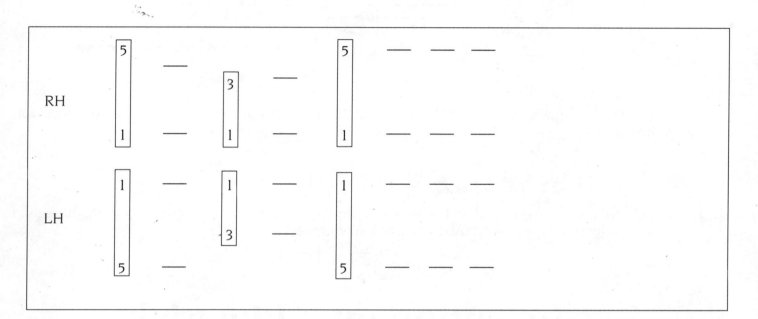

Exercise 7

RH   5   5   5   5   ——
         3   3   ——   4   4
                              2   2   ——   2   3
                                        1

RH   5   5   5
         3   3   ——   4
                    2   2   ——   3
                          1   1   —— —— ——

IMPROVISING

1. Play single tones on black keys only, alternating between left and right hand while your teacher or MIDI disk plays an accompaniment.

There are no wrong notes in improvisation. Feel free to experiment. Listen carefully and follow your teacher's or the disk's dynamic levels.

Teacher Accompaniment

Continue with varying dynamic levels.

2. Repeat the improvisation, and this time experiment with the effect of any of the pedals on your instrument.

PERFORMANCE

1. Your first performance will be based on the rhythms found within a limerick. You might listen to the sample performance on the MIDI disk before you play.

Invention on a Limerick

LYNN FREEMAN OLSON

	X √		**X** √
There	was a young	lady named	Bright (—)

	X √		**X** √
Whose	speed was far	faster than	light (—)

	X √	
She	went out one	day

	X √	
In a	relative	way

	X √		**X** √
And	returned home the	previous	night. (—)

Arthur Buller

Part 1 Solo

Play the rhythm of the words on single black keys. You may use various fingers and keys, but always shift back and forth from hand to hand, changing for each syllable.

Example:

```
        R     R   R           R
There was a young lady named Bright.
    L       L       L     L
```

Part 2 Solo

Play a steady pattern on a group of three black keys to match the √ marks shown. Play in the middle of the keyboard.

Part 3 Group

Play a steady drone pattern, lower on the keyboard. Create the drone by playing these keys simultaneously to match the **X** marks shown.

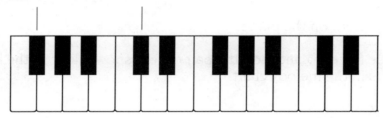

Create a longer piece of music.

a. Part 3 begin the drone.
b. Part 2 enter on the fifth drone sound.
c. Part 1 enter when it feels right.
d. Another solo: Take over Part 1 the second time through the limerick. Use keys higher on the piano.

Theme on a Curve

LYNN FREEMAN OLSON

2. Practice tapping on a flat surface while saying:

(RH)	TAP	TAP	TAP - hold
	TAP	TAP	TAP - hold
	TAP	TAP	TAP TAP
	TAP	TAP	TAP - hold

Repeat, using RH finger 2 and a light forearm motion.

Repeat, adding lateral motion while pointing to this keyboard melody chart, touching the indicated black keys.

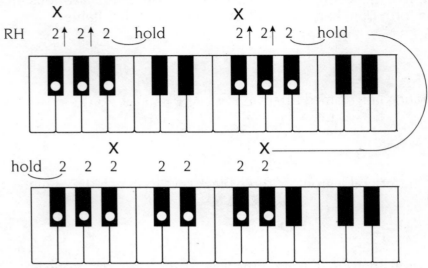

Next, play the same pattern on the piano.

Add a part for LH. Use fingers 5 and 1 on the pair of keys shown, low on the keyboard. Play and hold each time an **X** occurs in the melody chart.

Play again, using
another LH pair.

Theme on a Curve involves playing the melody three times, without stopping:

    a. with LH pair #1 — *f*
    b. with LH pair #2 — *p*
    c. with LH pair #1 — *f*

Create your own variation on black keys while keeping the LH as originally played.

3. In the center of the keyboard, find the following black-key groups:

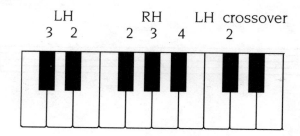

Amazing Grace

```
                                4                 4
                                                      ___
                                                       3
RH              ___              ___              ___
                 2               2                2
_____

LH        ___                                    ___
           3                               2      3
```

      A - ma - zing _____ grace, how sweet the sound,

```
                                                 _____
                                                 crossover LH 2
                     ___              ___
                      4                4
                                         ___
                                          3
RH              ___              ___
                 2               2
_____   etc.

LH        ___
           3
```

    That saved a _____ wretch, like me _____.

Teacher Part

Arranged by M. Hilley

2.

Simple Note Values/Key Names/ Black-Key Groups

LISTENING

Listen to the rhythms performed on the CD or MIDI disk and "tap back" after each example.

RHYTHM

♩	= Quarter note
♩	= Half note
♫	= Two eighth notes
o	= Whole note

1. Different note values are used as symbols to illustrate rhythms. It is important to understand the relationship of note durations. For example:

$$♩ = ♫$$

$$♩ = ♩ \ ♩ = ♫ \ ♫$$

(Also written: ♫♫)

$$o = ♩ \ ♩ = ♩ \ ♩ \ ♩ \ ♩$$

Tie   A curved line connecting two adjacent notes of the same pitch. The first note is played and held through the value of the second note.

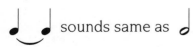 sounds same as ♩

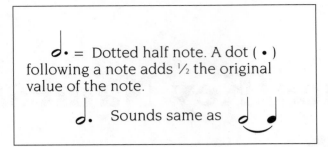 = Dotted half note. A dot (•)
following a note adds ½ the original
value of the note.

♩· Sounds same as ♩ ♩

2-2

Recorded examples on the CD or MIDI disk will demonstrate the following rhythms. Listen and tap back as you watch the note values.

1.

2.

3.

4.

5.

6.

7.

8.

Traditionally, note values are grouped together in equal sets marked off by vertical bar lines.

Example:

Stems extending upward are placed to the right of the note head.

Stems extending downward are placed to the left of the note head.

2. Tap the following rhythms on a flat surface. Use these syllables to maintain a steady pulse.

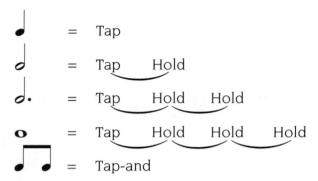

Use RH for upward-stemmed notes, LH for downward-stemmed notes.

Prepare by saying:

Pulse, Pulse, Ready, Tap

Pulse, Pulse, Ready, Tap

Pulse, Pulse, Pulse, Pulse, Ready, Tap

Ostinato   A short pattern of sounds
repeated continuously

---

3. Play each of the preceding rhythm patterns on the keyboard. Use various single black keys in each hand. Your teacher will provide an ostinato accompaniment. Before you begin, discuss the dynamics to be used.

4. Practice the following rhythm exercises. (When a box shows in place of a word, do not make any sound.)

a.	TAP	CLAP	TAP	CLAP
b.	TAP	CLAP	☐	CLAP
c.	TAP	☐	TAP	CLAP
d.	TAP	☐	☐	CLAP

2-3

Now perform the rhythm drills with the CD or MIDI disk as a background. Your teacher will call o the order.

TECHNIQUE

Tabletop exercises. With both hands on a flat surface, play the following examples using the indicated fingering. As a class, determine the speed for each example.

1.

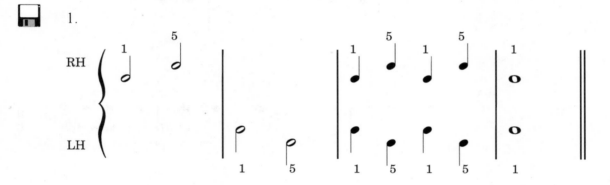

2.

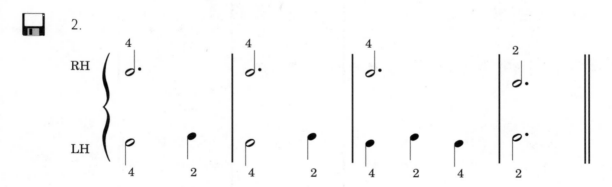

3.

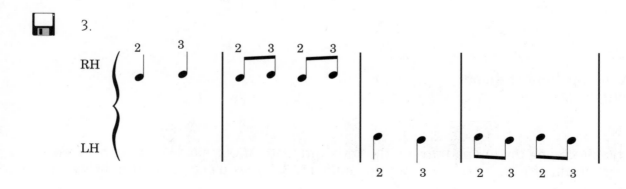

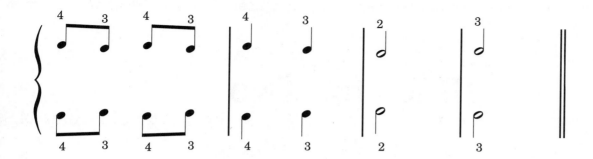

4. Return to the tabletop technique exercises in Chapter 1 (pp. 5–7). Your teacher will designate appropriate keyboard positions. Play the exercises with MIDI disk accompaniment.

THEORY

> **The Music Alphabet**   Seven letters, A B C D E F G, which are repeated over and over for the full range of the keyboard

1. Starting with the lowest A (to the left) on your keyboard, play from A to the highest key (to the right). Alternate finger 2 in the left and right hands. Use the following keyboard diagram as a guide.

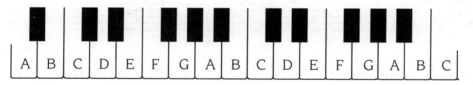

etc.

With what letter did you end? _____

Practice saying and playing the music alphabet forward and backward. Start with the *lowest* (to the left) A on the keyboard.

→
ABCDEFG—ABCDEFG—
←

Repeat several times on the keyboard starting with a different A each time.

2. The pattern of two and three black keys on the keyboard helps in locating specific white keys. For example, C is to the left of the two black keys; F is to the left of the three black keys.

3. The following piece has a feeling of 4. Listen to the teacher part, then add the indicated fill-in on the second time through.

Blues for Two

LYNN FREEMAN OLSON

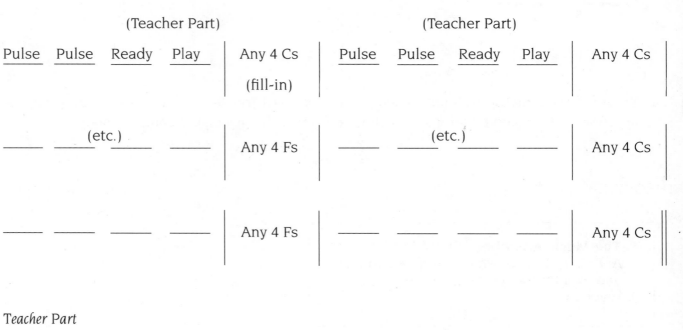

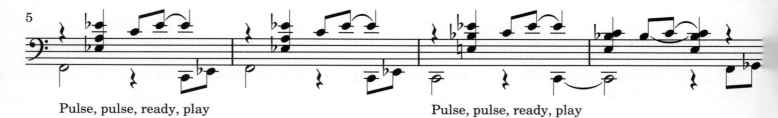

4. The CD will give a letter name. Using the rhythm below, answer with the two letter names that follow each given letter.

For example, you will hear:

Pulse, pulse, begin   A ___ ___

Following A, you would say: "B"   "C"

Begin example 2-4 on the CD.

5. The CD will give a letter name. Repeat the exercise as in 4, this time naming the letters backward from each given letter.

For example, following A, you would say "G"   "F".

6. *Tabletop exercises.* Using a flat surface, practice the following examples as the CD or MIDI disk provides a background.

a. Pulse, pulse, ready, play

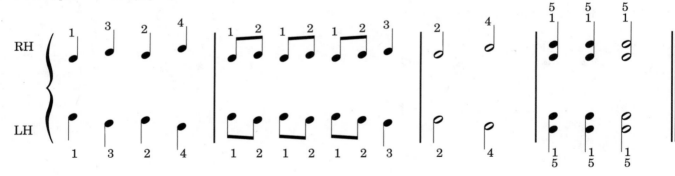

b. Pulse, pulse, pulse, pulse, ready, play

7. Name the final pitch in each pattern. Think the intervening pitches.

Example:

Pulse, pulse, ready, begin:

C   (D)   (E)   (F) | G

Move upward through the pitches.

Pulse, pulse, ready, begin:

A — — — | —

G — — — | —

E — — — | —

B — — — | —

F — — — | —

D — — — | —

Now play all five pitches of each pattern and name only the starting and ending letters as you play. Use fingers 5 4 3 2 1 of the left hand. Your teacher will provide an accompaniment.

Teacher Accompaniment

mf detached

8. Name the final pitch in each pattern. Think the intervening pitches. Move *downward* through the pitches. Use the same rhythm as item 7:

Pulse, pulse, ready, begin:

D	(C)	(B)	(A)	G
C	—	—	—	F
A	—	—	—	—
E	—	—	—	—
B	—	—	—	—
G	—	—	—	—

Now play all five pitches of each pattern. Use fingers 5 4 3 2 1 of the right hand. Your teacher (or the MIDI disk) will provide an accompaniment.

Teacher Accompaniment

READING

In the following two pieces, group 1 performs the RH part (part 1); group 2 performs the LH part (part 2). Repeat each piece once, switching parts at the repetition.

Song for September

LYNN FREEMAN OLSO

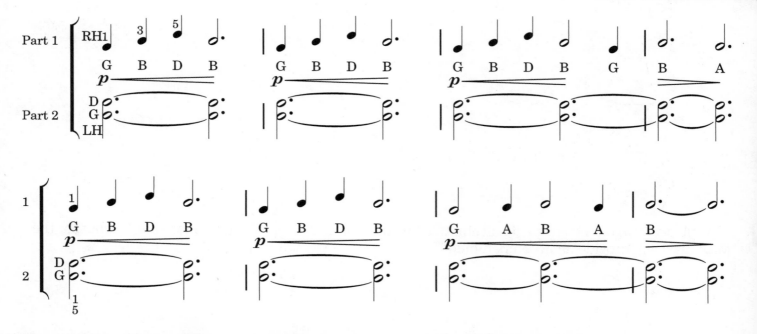

Rain

LYNN FREEMAN OLSON

IMPROVISING

1. Use the following keys to improvise as your teacher provides an accompaniment.

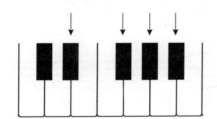

Teacher Accompaniment

2. Use the same pitches as item 1 to play answers to your teacher's musical questions. Remember, these are improvised answers, not echoes. Close your book as you listen and respond.

Branches

LYNN FREEMAN OLSON

Connected

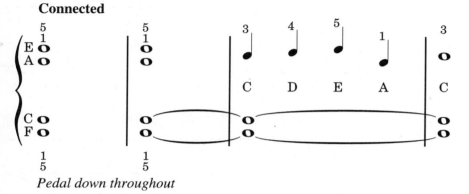

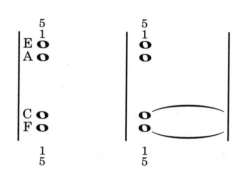

Pedal down throughout

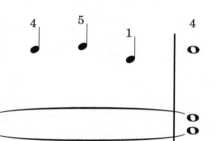

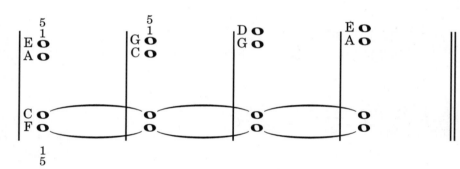

Old School Song

LYNN FREEMAN OLSON

Very lively

Swing Low, Sweet Chariot

Spiritu...
Arranged by M. Hill...

(Teacher Part) | (etc.)
— — — — | — — — —
Swing low,   sweet | char- i ot, ___

					5	5 — — —
			3	3		
1	1	1	1			
Com - in' for to car - ry me | home; _____

(Teacher Part) | (etc.)
— — — — | — — — —
Swing low,   sweet | char- i ot, ___

| | | | 3 | 3 | | |
| 1 | 1 | 1 | 1 | | 2 | 1 — — |
Com - in' for to car - ry me | home; ___ I

(Teacher Part) | (etc.)
— — — — | — — — —
looked o-ver Jordan and | what did I see?___

					5	5 — —
			3	3		
1	1	1	1			
Com - in' for to car - ry me | home; ___ A

(Teacher Part) | (etc.)
— — — — | — — — —
band of   an-gels | com - in' aft-ter me,

| | | | 3 | 3 | | |
| 1 | 1 | 1 | 1 | | 2 | 1 — — — |
Com - in' for to car - ry me | home. _____

Repeat first two lines

Teacher Part

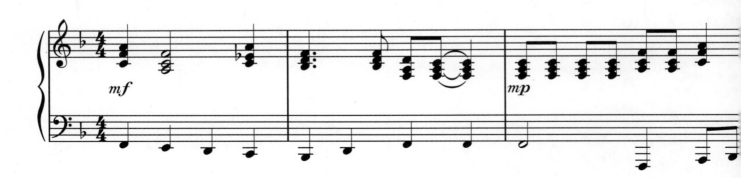

Nobody Knows

American

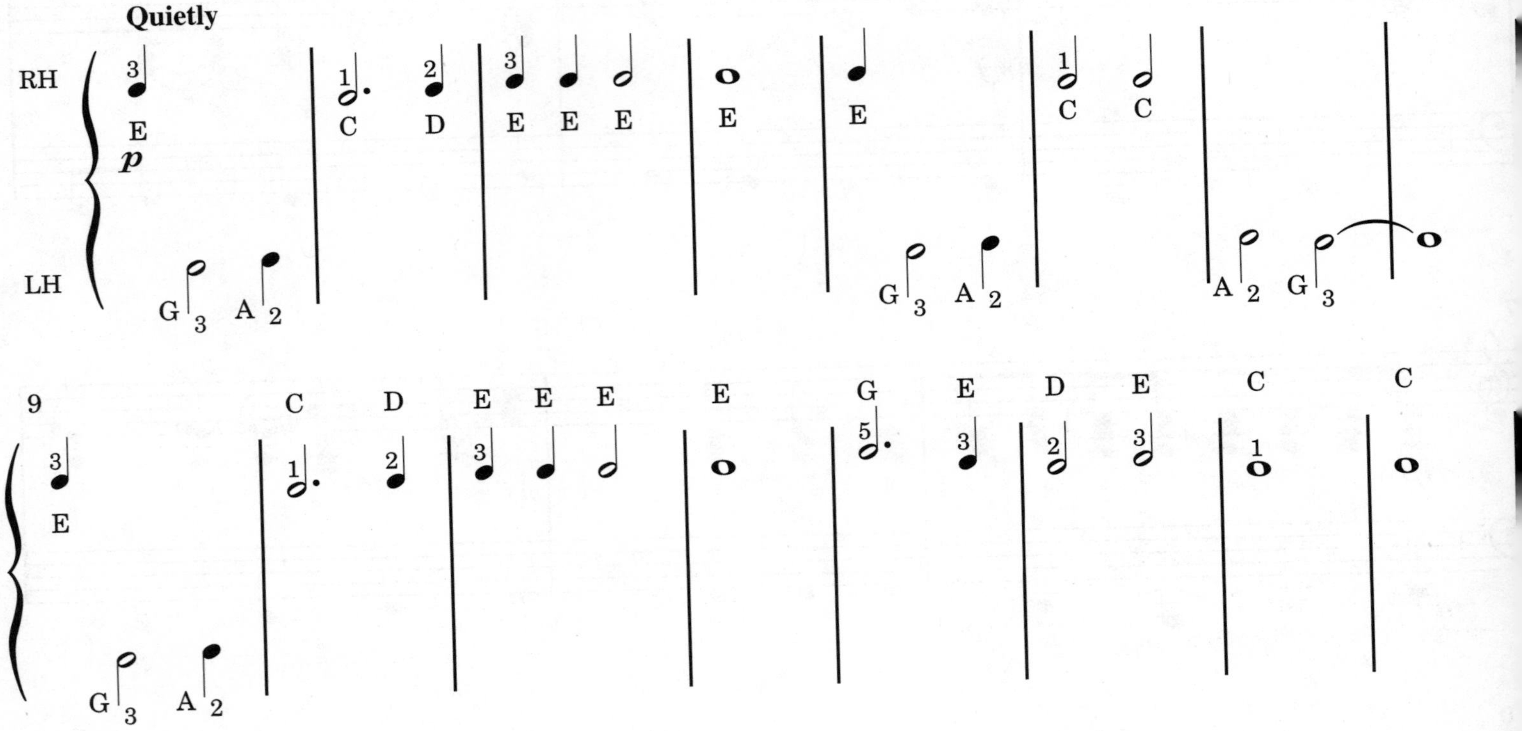

Quietly

RH
3 E *p*
1 C . 2 D 3 E E E E E 1 C C

LH
G 3 A 2 G 3 A 2 A 2 G 3 o

9
3 E
C D E E E E G E D E C C
1 . 2 3 o 5 . 3 2 3 1 o o

G 3 A 2

Teacher Chord Chart:

C	F	C	Amin
C	F	Dmin7	G7
C	F	C	A7
Dmin7	G7	F	C

3. Play through *Romantic Melody* twice. Think carefully about the indicated dynamics.

Romantic Melody

LYNN FREEMAN OLSON

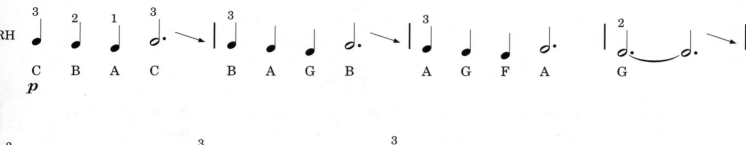

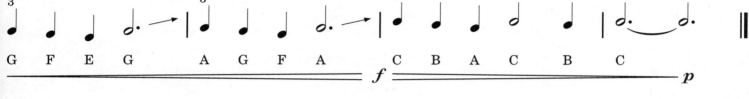

Teacher Accompaniment

WRITING

1. Copy the following rhythm patterns in the space provided below each. Tap each rhythm after you have copied it.

a.

RH

b.

LH

c.

RH
LH

2. Furnish the missing note values for *Swing Low, Sweet Chariot*.

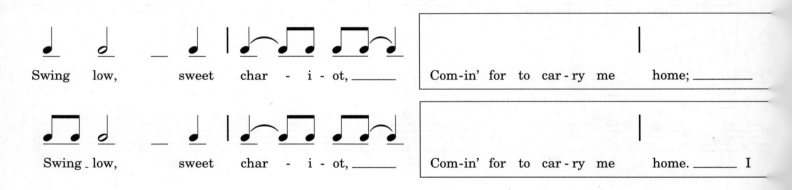

Swing   low,   sweet   char - i - ot, _____   Com-in' for to car-ry me   home; _____

Swing _ low,   sweet   char - i - ot, _____   Com-in' for to car-ry me   home. _____ I

2

looked o - ver Jor-dan and what did I see? ____ | Com-in' for to car-ry me home: ____ A

band _ of an - gels com - in' af - ter me. ____ | Com-in' for to car-ry me home. _____

3.

Meter Signatures/Rests/Line and Space Notes/Steps and Skips/ Seconds and Thirds

LISTENING

3-1

1. Listen to the rhythms performed on the CD or MIDI disk and tap back after each example. Directions will be given before each example.

2. Place the CD on 3-1 and listen again, this time "playing back" the rhythms on the following pitches:

G   A   B   C   D

Experiment with different orders of these pitches. Alternate hands between exercises.

RHYTHM

1. Meter signatures are used to describe the rhythmic organization of music.

Measure   A set of equal pulses marked off by bar lines

Example: ♩ ♩ | ♩ ♩

Meter Signature (also called Time Signature)   A symbol used to indicate the number of pulses (beats) contained in a measure of music (top number). It also indicates the type of note value that will receive a single pulse (bottom number).

Example: $\frac{2}{4}$ — two pulses or beats in each measure. With this meter signature, a quarter note receives one beat.

As a class, discuss the meaning of the following meter signatures:

$\frac{2}{4}$ $\frac{3}{4}$ $\frac{4}{4}$ $\frac{5}{4}$ $\frac{6}{4}$ $\frac{2}{2}$

2. To ensure steady rhythm, it is best to count aloud. For further security, rhythms should be subdivided on the basis of the smallest note value used.

Example:

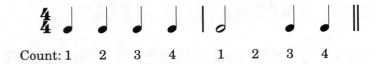

Count: 1   2   3   4   1   2   3   4

Count: 1 & 2 & 3 & 4 &   1 & 2 & 3 & 4 &

3. Furnish meter signatures for the following rhythm exercises, then tap as you count aloud. Be certain to subdivide when necessary.

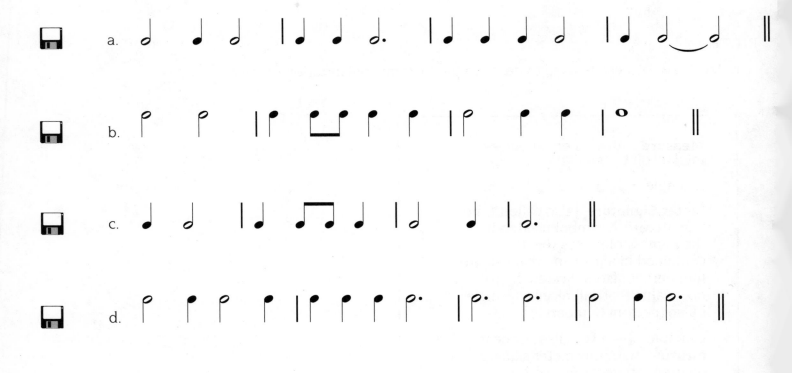

4. In music, silence is as important as sound. Symbols used to indicate silence are called *rests*.

> 𝄽   Quarter rest (equivalent in duration to the quarter note)
>
> ▬   Half rest (equivalent in duration to the half note)
>
> ▬   Whole rest (equivalent in duration to the whole note; also equals a whole measure of rest no matter what the meter)

Tap the following as you count aloud.

a.

b.

c. Choose a partner and tap. Switch parts and tap again.

Choose a partner again—or keep the one you had!

e. Tap this alternating rhythm pattern by yourself. Tap the RH on one surface (desktop, music rack) and the LH on another surface (leg, head).

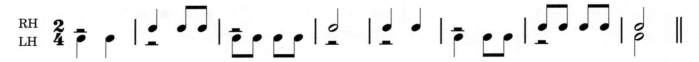

3-2

5. Count aloud as you tap the following rhythms. The CD or MIDI disks will provide a background.

a.

b.

c.

TECHNIQUE

Tabletop exercises. Practice the following examples on a flat surface. The CD or MIDI disk will set the tempo.

1.

2.

3.

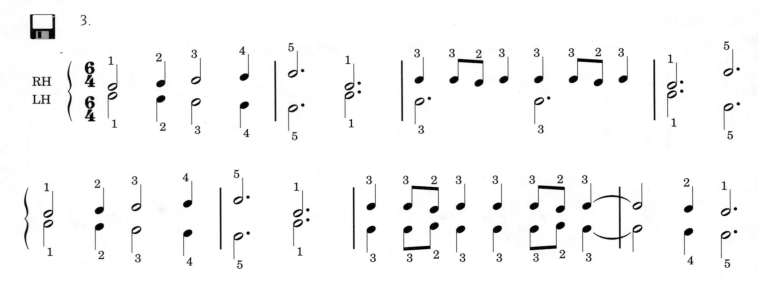

Repeat the last example on the keyboard. Use the indicated beginning pitches and follow the finger patterns.

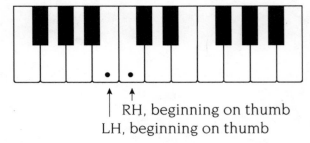

RH, beginning on thumb
LH, beginning on thumb

4. Return to the tabletop technique in Chapter 2 (pp. 21–22). Determine beginning pitches and ove range and play with the recorded backgrounds.

THEORY

3-4

1. The CD will call for random pitches to be played on the keyboard. Use a wide range and alternate between the hands.

Example:

```
            /  /   /      /  /  /   /
CD:         1  2  play an A  |1  2  3  A
                  student plays    ↑
```

3-5

2. The CD will give a key name. In rhythm, answer with the TWO pitches that follow, wait a measure and then play all three pitches.

Example:

```
            /  /    /     /    /   /
CD:         1  2  begin | F  "G"  "A"
                             ↑    ↑
                            say
            /  /   /    /   /   /
            1  2  play | F   G   A
                        ↑   ↑   ↑
                       play
```

READING

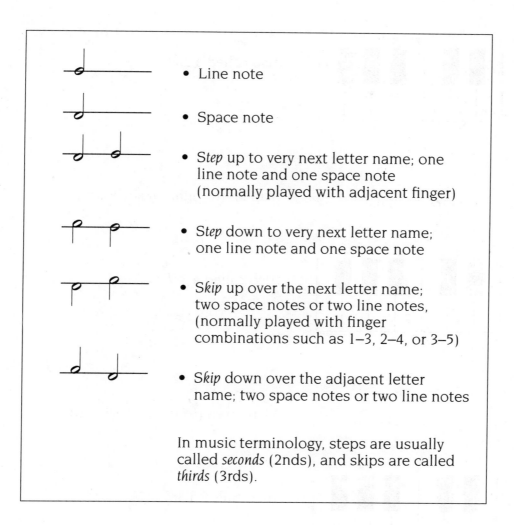

- Line note

- Space note

- *Step* up to very next letter name; one line note and one space note (normally played with adjacent finger)

- *Step* down to very next letter name; one line note and one space note

- *Skip* up over the next letter name; two space notes or two line notes, (normally played with finger combinations such as 1–3, 2–4, or 3–5)

- *Skip* down over the adjacent letter name; two space notes or two line notes

In music terminology, steps are usually called *seconds* (2nds), and skips are called *thirds* (3rds).

1. Note heads in music are placed either on a line or in the space above or below the line. The arrangement of notes as line or space notes determines the direction you will move on the keyboard.

Examples:

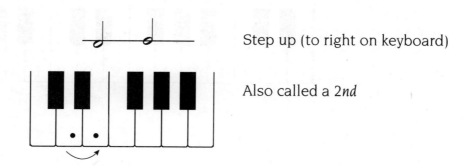

Step up (to right on keyboard)

Also called a *2nd*

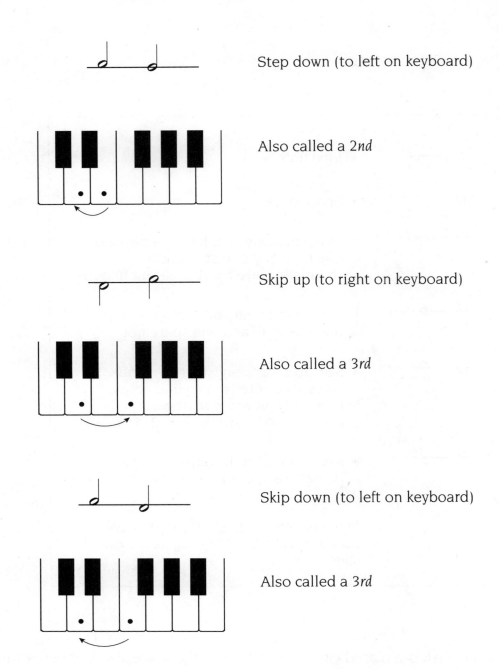

Step down (to left on keyboard)

Also called a *2nd*

Skip up (to right on keyboard)

Also called a *3rd*

Skip down (to left on keyboard)

Also called a *3rd*

Practice playing the following examples of skips and steps (seconds and thirds) on the keyboard.

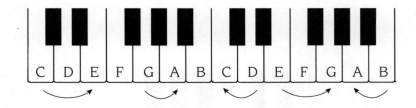

2. Logical fingering is one of the most important components in reading piano music. Stepwise motion in music usually calls for consecutive fingering (1, 2, 3), whereas skips, or thirds, call for a skip in fingering (2–4, 3–5, 1–3).

Discuss possible fingerings for the following examples and play. Count aloud to ensure a steady pulse.

a. Begin on E

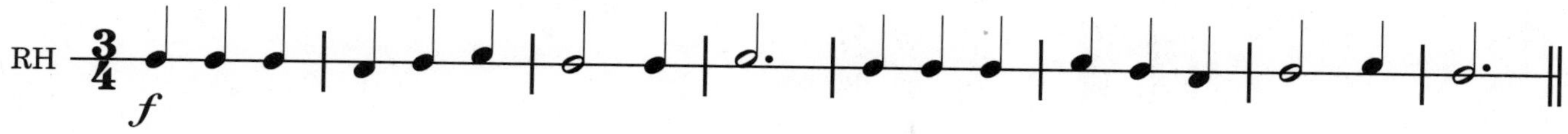

b. Begin on A

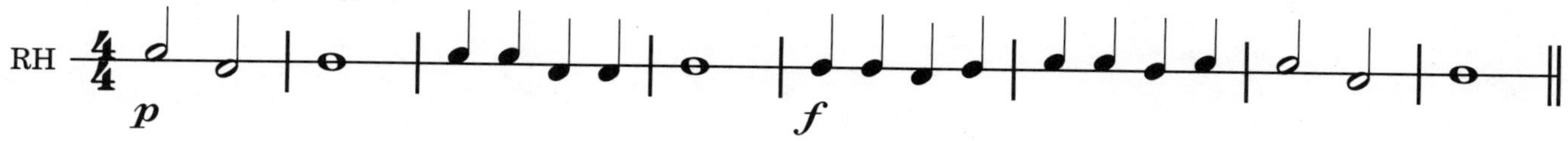

c. Begin on G

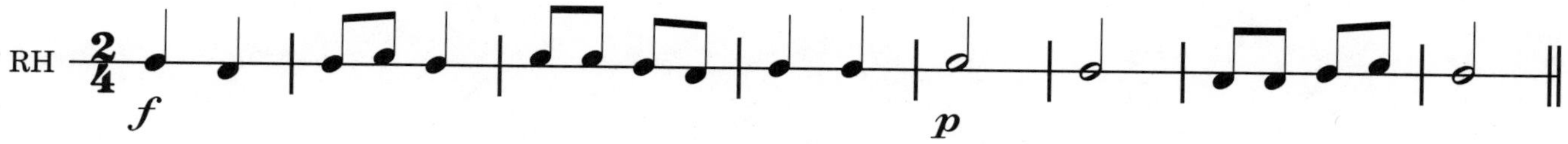

d. Begin on F

e. Begin on C

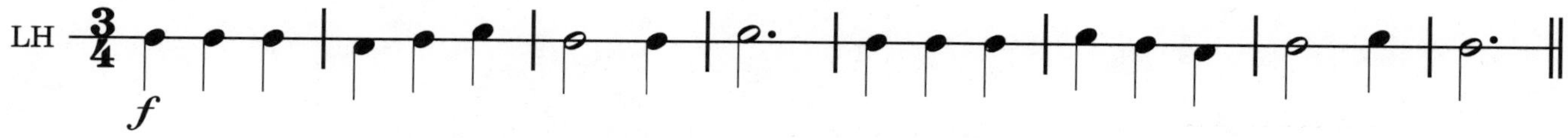

 f. Begin on G

 g. Begin on F

 h. Begin on B

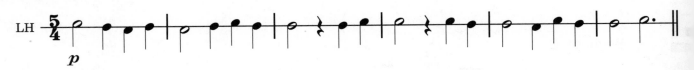

3. Carefully study the following examples.

 • Step up (to the right on the keyboard)

 • Step down (to the left on the keyboard)

 • Skip up (to the right on the keyboard)

 • Skip down (to the left on the keyboard)

4. Determine a logical fingering and play.

a. Begin on F

b. Begin on E

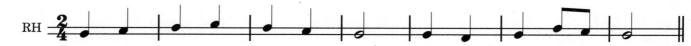

c. Begin on F

d. Begin on D

(Return to page 7, Exercise 7, and complete transcribing the notes to the two-line staff.)

Transcribe To make a written copy. In music, a "transcription" can mean to adapt a piece for an instrument or voice for which the piece was not originally written.

Interval The distance from one key (or note) to another

5. From D to F is an interval of a third. It spans three letter names.

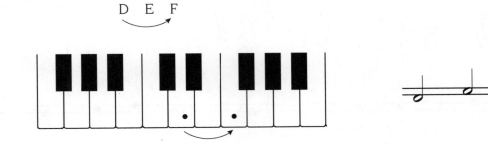

From D to E is an interval of a second. It spans two letter names.

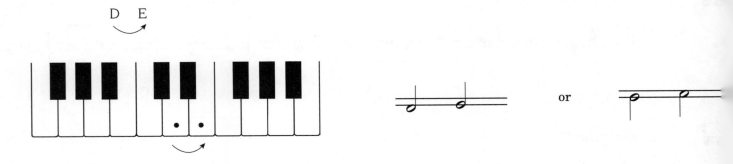

From G to E is an interval of a third. It spans three letter names.

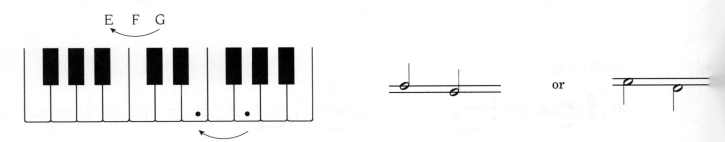

From D to C is an interval of a second. It spans two letter names.

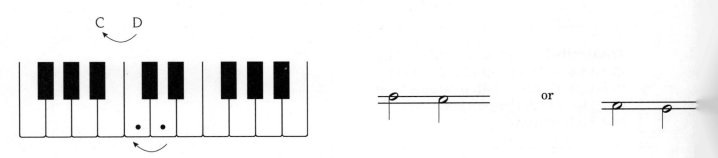

6. Use the music alphabet as a reference.

- Begin with the lowest A and say letter names up in thirds.
- Begin with the lowest B and say letter names up in thirds.
- Begin with the highest C and say letter names down in thirds.
- Begin with the highest B and say letter names down in thirds.

Now go back and play the above exercises. Use alternating hands, finger 2 in each hand.

7. Play through the following interval chains:

- RH Position: D E F G A

    Play: D
         up a third
         down a second
         up a second
         down a third   You ended on _____

- LH Position: D E F G A

    Play: D
         up a third
         down a second
         up a third
         up a second
         down a third   You ended on _____

- RH Position: G A B C D
    Your teacher will dictate intervals.

- LH Position: G A B C D
    Your teacher will dictate intervals.

48

IMPROVISING

1. Improvise by repeating this two-measure rhythm. Use the five white keys indicated. Your teacher will provide an accompaniment.

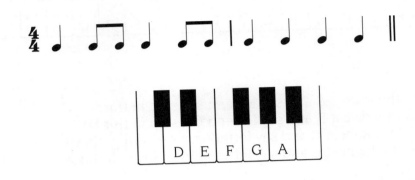

Teacher Accompaniment

mp

etc.

PERFORMANCE

Stomp Dance

LYNN FREEMAN OLSO

MARTHA HILL

Firmly

RH

f

Teacher Accompaniment

f

3

Begin on E

Wind Song

LYNN FREEMAN OLSON

Swaying

Teacher Accompaniment

MARTHA HILLEY

Legato throughout

Begin on G

Catfish

American
Arranged by Lynn Freeman Olson

Lively

Teacher Accompaniment

MARTHA HILLEY

Round Dance

LYNN FREEMAN OLSON

Lullaby

LYNN FREEMAN OLSO

MARTHA HILLEY

Teacher Accompaniment

Teacher Part (Optional)

MARTHA HILL

Bim Bom

Arranged by Martha Hilley

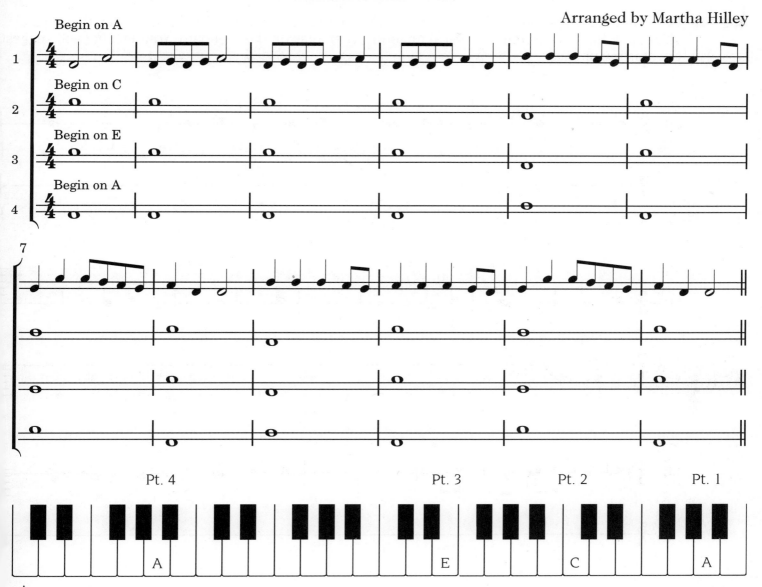

Lowest C on keyboard

Teacher Accompaniment (Optional)

WRITING

1. Copy the following "directional" rhythms in the space allowed. After copying, tap each rhythm as you count aloud. Determine a logical fingering, then play on the keyboard. Your teacher will suggest the starting pitches.

a.

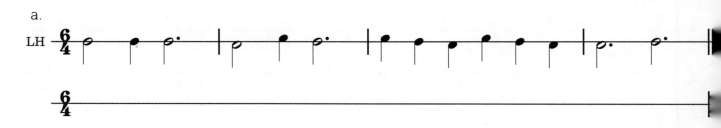

b.

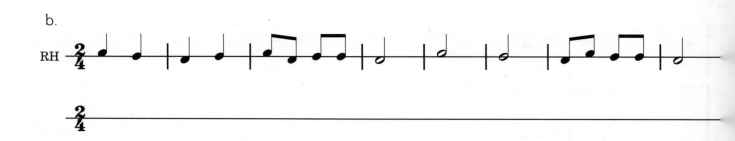

c.

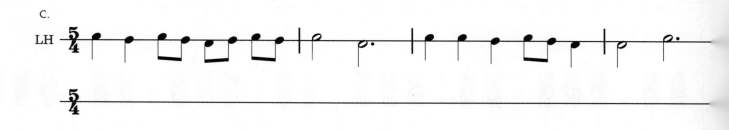

d.

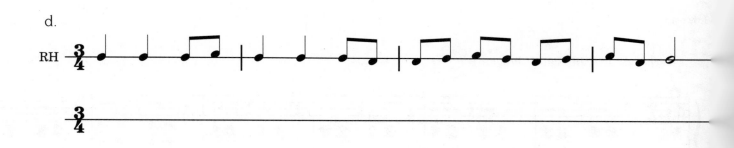

e.

4.

Recap

PERFORMANCE

Evening Song

LYNN FREEMAN OLSON

Morning Has Broken

Arranged by Martha Hilley

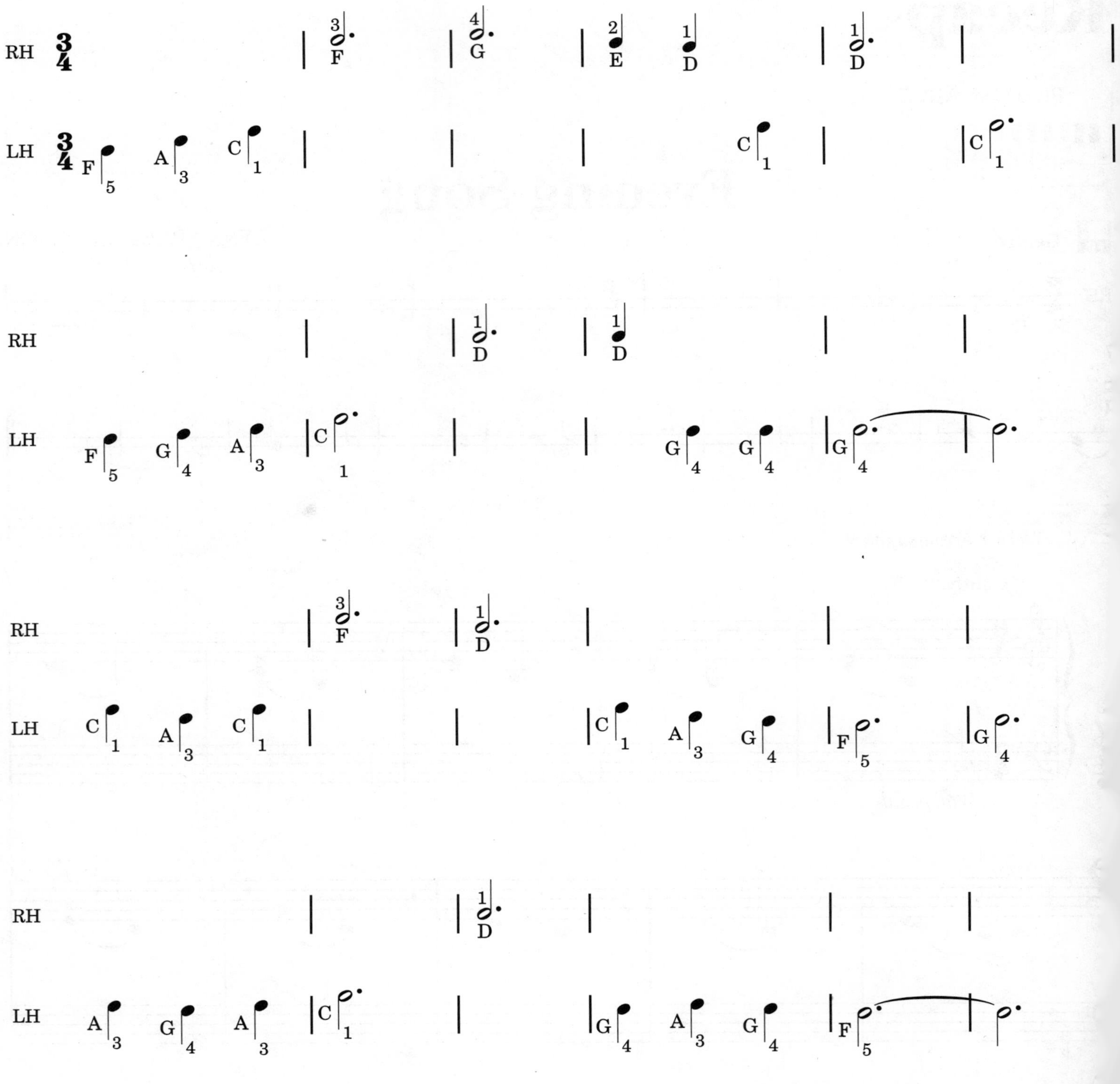

4

Morning Has Broken

Teacher Accompaniment

Arranged by Martha Hilley

Barcarolle

JACQUES OFFENBACH
(1819–1880)
Arranged by Lynn Freeman Olson

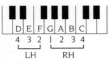

Teacher Accompaniment

4

He's Got the Whole World

Spiritual
Arranged by Martha Hilley

Teacher Accompaniment

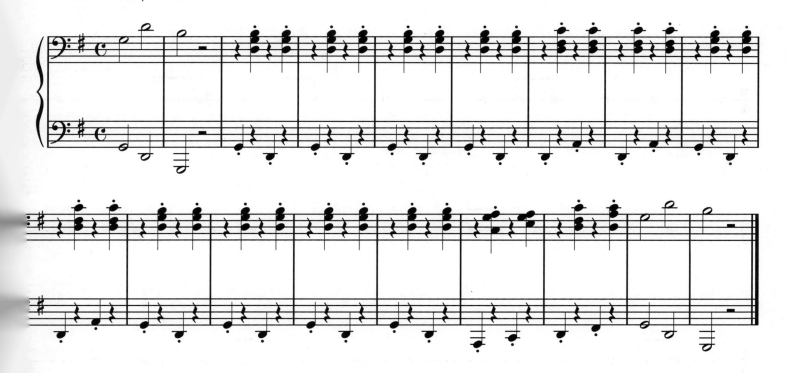

TERMINOLOGY REVIEW

Discuss the following musical terms:

- Music alphabet
- Line note/space note
- Step/skip
- Dynamics
- Note values/rest values
- Meter signatures
- Measure/bar line
- Step direction
- Tie
- Ostinato
- Transcribe
- Intervals

WRITING REVIEW

1. Add bar lines to the following rhythm examples.

2. Circle the ONE INCORRECT measure in each of the following examples. How would you correct the error in each item?

a.

b.

c.

d.

3. Finish this melody any way you like, then play.

Begin on C

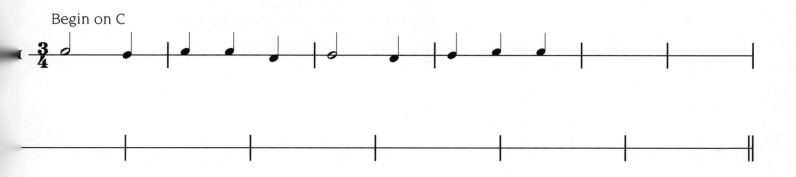

5.

Treble and Bass/Grand Staff/ Fourths and Fifths/Half Steps and Whole Steps/Sharps and Flats

LISTENING

1. Your teacher will play five-tone melodies that move up (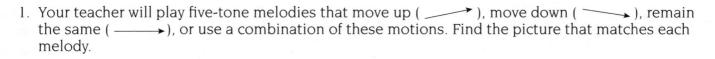), move down (———→), remain the same (———→), or use a combination of these motions. Find the picture that matches each melody.

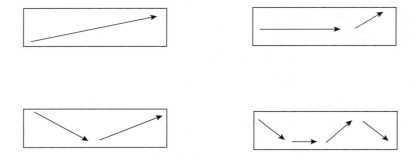

2. Your teacher will play from the following patterns. After hearing each pattern, you will imitate it. Close your book and listen carefully for instructions.

Teacher announces, "Begin RH finger 2 on F. Listen."

Teacher announces, "Begin RH finger 5 on G. Listen."

Teacher announces, "Begin RH finger 4 on F. Listen."

Teacher announces, "Begin LH finger 1 on D. Listen."

Teacher announces, "Begin RH finger 2 on D. Listen."

Teacher announces, "Begin LH finger 3 on F. Listen."

RHYTHM

1. Tap and count the following rhythms that use ties.

2. Discuss the dynamic levels before performing *Tap It Out*.

Tap It Out

LYNN FREEMAN OLSON

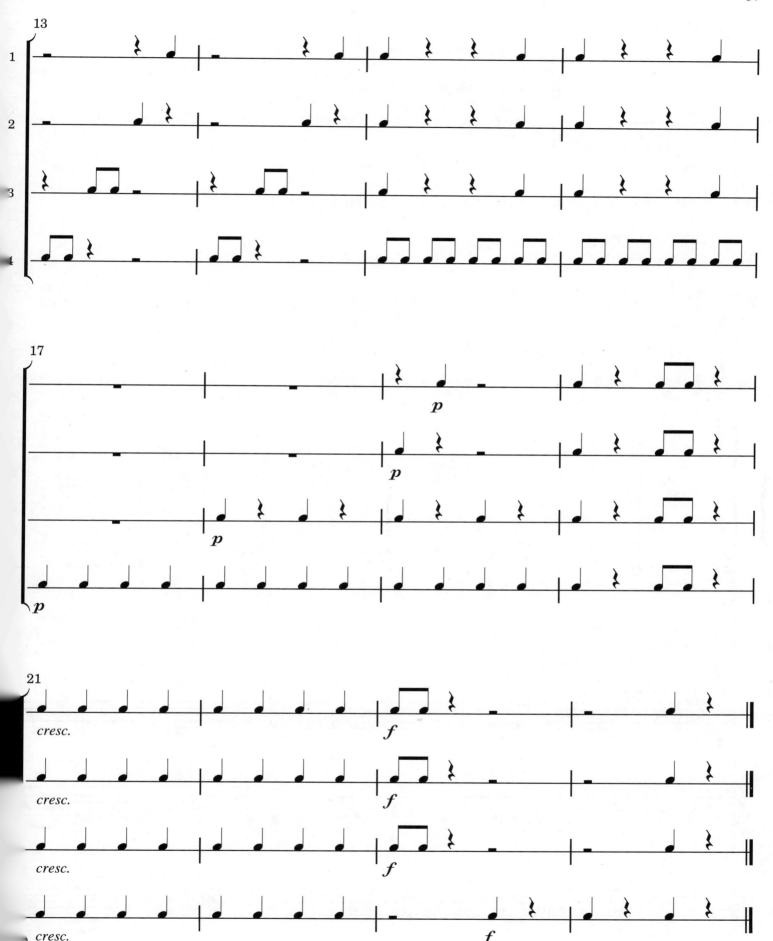

TECHNIQUE

Repeat Sign Return to the beginning and play again, or return to the previous repeat sign and play again.

1. Play the following accompaniment as your teacher provides a melody.

Student Accompaniment

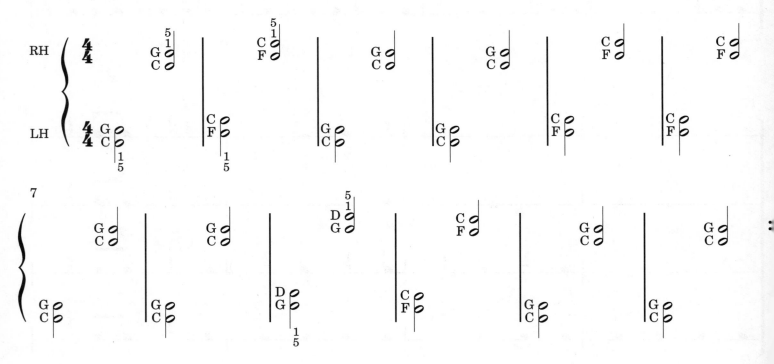

Teacher Melody

2. Return to the tabletop technique exercises in Chapter 3 (pp. 39–40). Use the white keys from A to E for item 1, white keys from G to D for item 2, and white keys from D to A for item 3. Play along with the MIDI disk background.

THEORY

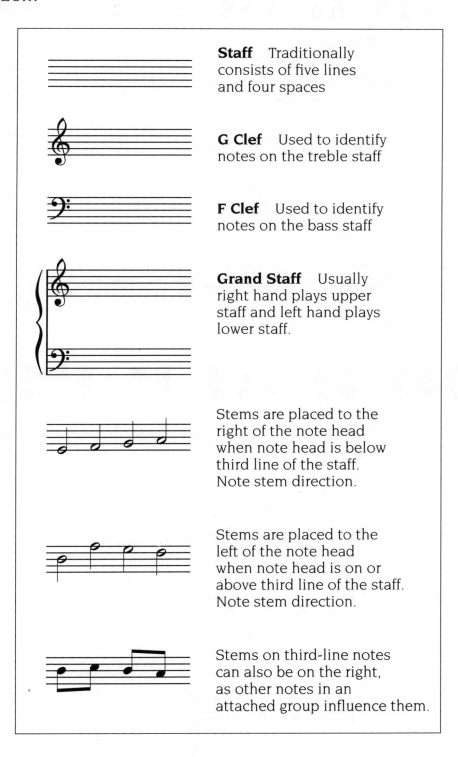

Staff   Traditionally consists of five lines and four spaces

G Clef   Used to identify notes on the treble staff

F Clef   Used to identify notes on the bass staff

Grand Staff   Usually right hand plays upper staff and left hand plays lower staff.

Stems are placed to the right of the note head when note head is below third line of the staff. Note stem direction.

Stems are placed to the left of the note head when note head is on or above third line of the staff. Note stem direction.

Stems on third-line notes can also be on the right, as other notes in an attached group influence them.

Relationship of Piano Keyboard to Grand Staff

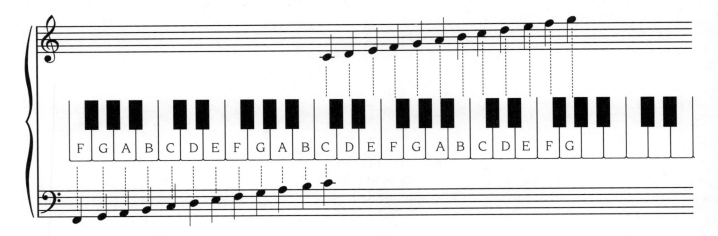

1. Use the G clef and F clef landmarks to locate pitches on the keyboard.

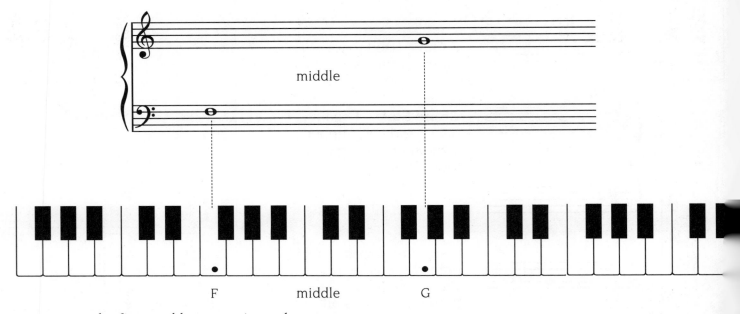

1. Name the first and last note in each measure.

In each measure, select an appropriate beginning finger and play. Name the notes as you play. Notic intervals of 2nds and 3rds.

2. Landmark Cs will help to increase your keyboard range.

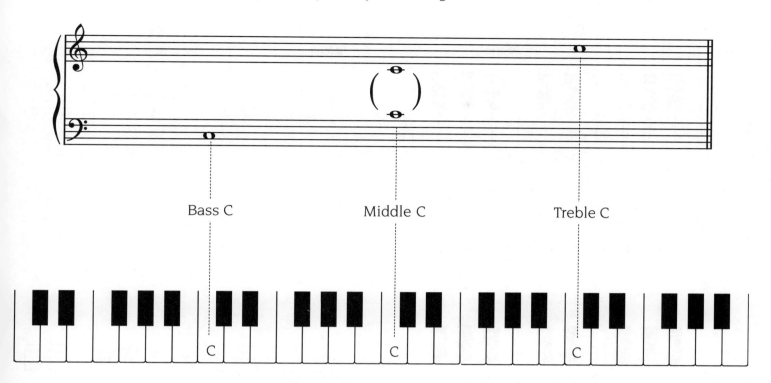

Bass C   Middle C   Treble C

Name the first and last note in each measure.

For each measure, select an appropriate beginning finger and play. Name the notes as you play. At each double bar, you may wish to take time to determine the next position. If so, add one measure of rest before each new example.

3. From C to G is an interval of a 5th.

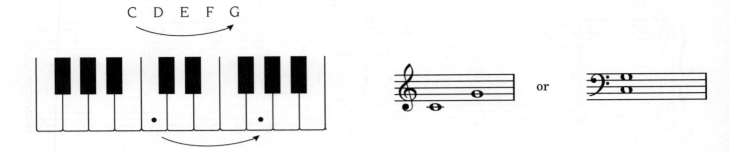

From C to F is an interval of a 4th.

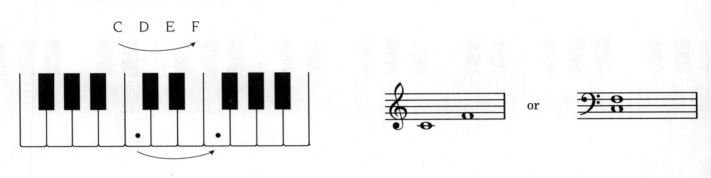

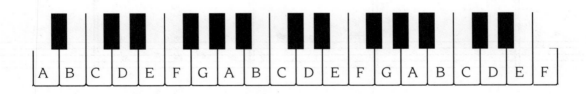

Use the music alphabet as a reference.
- Begin with the lowest A and say letter names up in 5ths.
- Begin with the lowest B and say letter names up in 5ths.
- Begin with the highest C and say letter names down in 4ths.
- Begin with the highest B and say letter names down in 4ths.

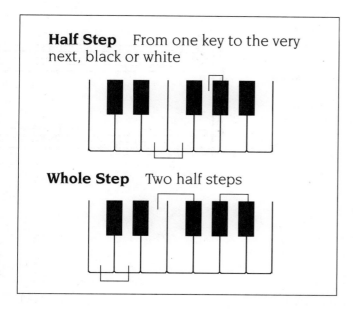

Half Step From one key to the very next, black or white

Whole Step Two half steps

4. On the keyboard provided, mark the half steps that occur from white key to white key.

Play these half steps on your keyboard. They are called "natural" half steps.

♯ **Sharp** Raises a note one half step

♭ **Flat** Lowers a note one half step

The effect of a sharp or flat lasts through the measure.

5. Play the sharp for each given key.

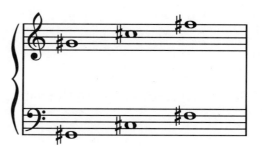

6. Play the flat for each given key

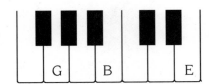

| ♮ **Natural**   This sign cancels the effect of a sharp or a flat. |

7. Play the natural key and then the sharp key as shown.

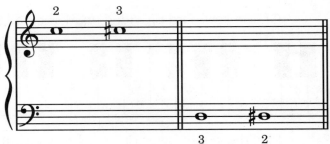

8. Play the sharp key and then play the natural key as shown.

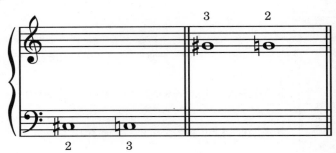

9. Play the natural key and then the flat key.

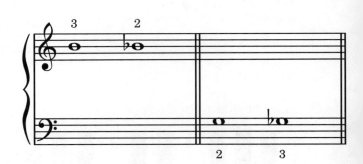

10. Play the flat key and then the natural key.

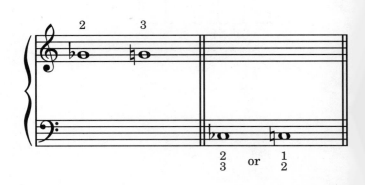

READING

1. Play these interval studies. Something about them should seem familiar. Also, notice the suggested beginning fingering.

2. *Reading flashes.* Look carefully at the following two-measure examples. Your teacher will announce the order in which they are to be played; reading will be nonstop from one to the next.

Position

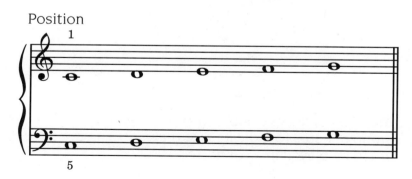

Slur A curved line above or below a group of notes to indicate that they are to be played in a connected manner

3. Play the following revision of *Romantic Melody* as your teacher accompanies. Pay particular attention to slurs.

Romantic Melody Revisited

LYNN FREEMAN OLSON

Teacher Accompaniment

IMPROVISING

Broken Intervals   Notes played one after the other; also called *melodic intervals*

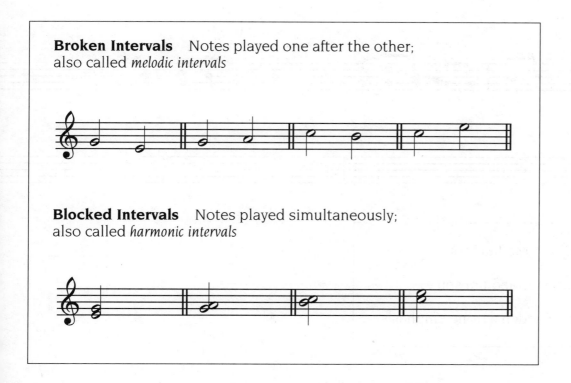

Blocked Intervals   Notes played simultaneously; also called *harmonic intervals*

1. Play the following broken intervals (melodic intervals).

2. Play the following blocked intervals (harmonic intervals).

3. In a $\frac{4}{4}$ meter, improvise four-measure answers to your teacher's questions. Before beginning each example, establish a keyboard position the same as your teacher's.

Melodic intervals

Harmonic intervals

Your choice

mf	*Mezzo forte*	Medium loud
mp	*Mezzo piano*	Medium soft
>	**Accent**	Sudden, strong emphasis

3. This popular folk tune uses both melodic and harmonic intervals.

Clap-Hands Dance

Mexican
Arranged by Lynn Freeman Olson

WRITING

1. Use the blank score below to transcribe all parts of *Bim Bom* (p. 51). Trade books and perform the ensemble using a classmate's score.

Bim Bom

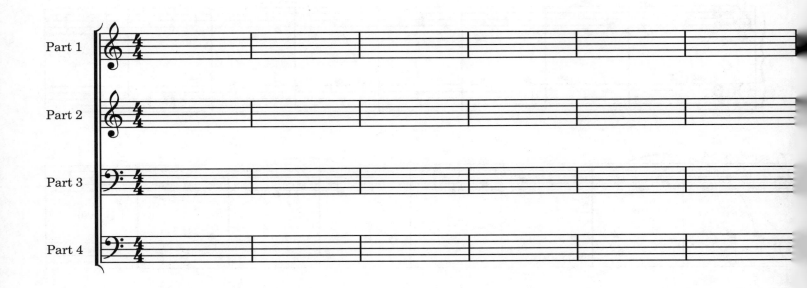

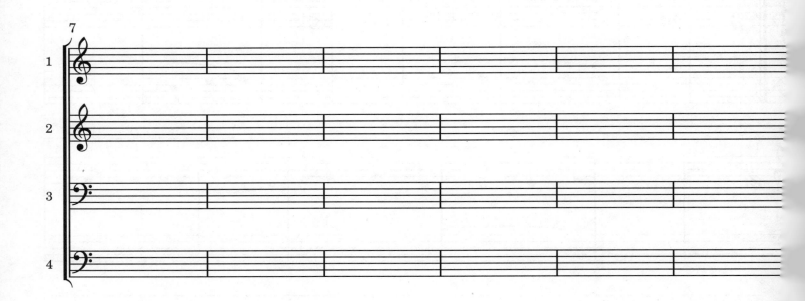

2. Use the blank score below to transcribe the student part of *Morning Has Broken* (p. 56). Play from your score as your teacher accompanies.

Morning Has Broken

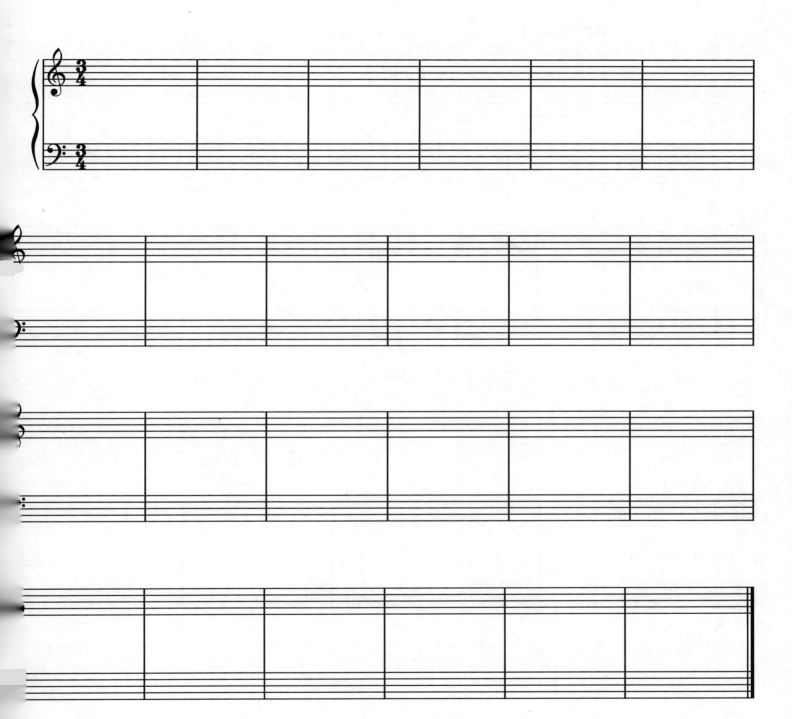

3. Copy the following grand staff examples and then play each from your manuscript.

6.

Dotted Rhythms/Phrases

LISTENING

6-1

1. You will hear four musical examples on the CD or MIDI disk. Listen carefully and identify each example from the music shown below.

a.

Traditional

b.

WOLFGANG AMADEUS MOZART
(1756–1791)

c.

FRANZ SCHUBERT
(1797–1828)

d.

GEORGE M. COHAN
(1878–1942)

9

Phrase   Musical "sentence" that may or may not be indicated by a curved line. Phrases may vary in length.

2. Listen to the four musical examples again. As a class, determine the phrase lengths in each. Mark the phrases in the music.

Andante   Moderately walking

Allegro   Bright, moderately fast

Lento   Quite slow

Vivace   Lively, very fast

6-2

3. Listen carefully to the four musical examples on the CD or MIDI disk. On a replay, determine which piece is an example of *Andante*, which is *Allegro*, which is *Lento*, and which is *Vivace*.

RHYTHM

1. Tap and count the following rhythm examples.

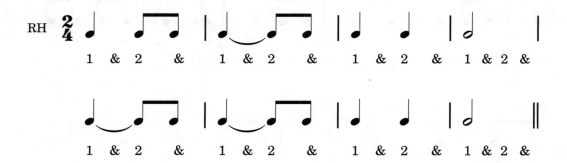

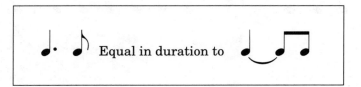

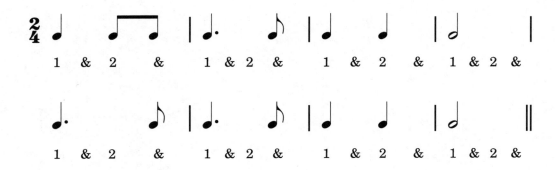

2. Choose different surfaces to "perform" these rhythms.

TECHNIQUE

6-3

1. *Tabletop technique.* Practice the following exercises on a flat surface. The CD and MIDI disk will set the tempo. Count aloud.

a.

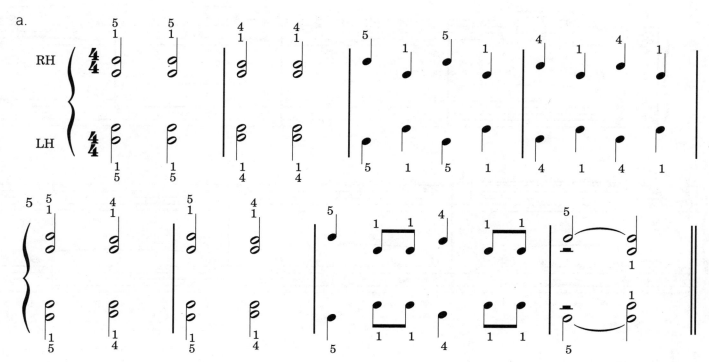

b.

c.

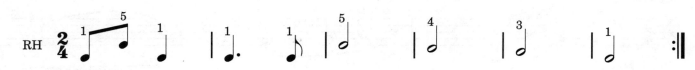

2. Name the beginning pitches of each example. Determine fingering and play.

a.

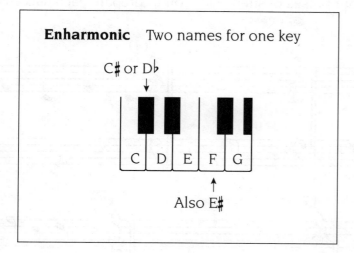

Enharmonic   Two names for one key

C♯ or D♭

Also E♯

Play the sharp key for each given key; then repeat, playing the flat key for each given key.

READING

1. *Reading flashes.* Look carefully at the following examples. Your teacher will announce the order in which they are to be played. There will be four pulses of silence for you to prepare each successive example.

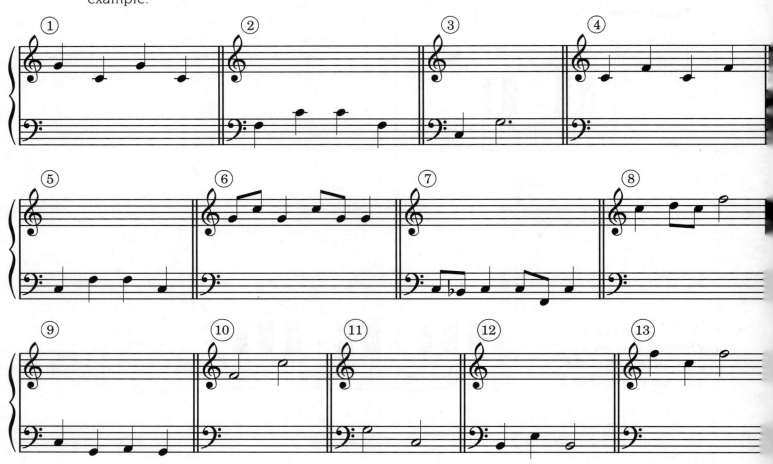

2. Determine fingering and play.

Shifting Light

LYNN FREEMAN OLSO

3. Name the following notes. Proceed steadily, feeling four beats to a note. Think treble clef.

4. Name the same notes again, this time allowing only two beats per note. If you have no trouble doing this, turn your book upside down and do it once again. Think treble clef the first time and bass clef on the repeat.

5. Return to the notes in item 3. PLAY each note, four beats to a note. This time think bass clef. Place a mark by the notes on which you hesitated. Practice the ones that you marked.

   Play again, this time thinking treble clef. Place a mark by the ones you hesitated on and practice those again.

   If you have no trouble with four beats to a note, repeat the exercise using two beats to a note.

6. Follow the same steps as in items 3 and 5. These will take more "bench time!"

(Bass)

(Treble)

IMPROVISING

1 Add all black-key melodic improvisations above the following black-key ostinato patterns.

Now improvise your own black-key ostinato with melody.

2. Improvise a piece with three sections.

Section A: Use whole steps that are entirely on black keys; use pedal as in *Branches* on page 27; involve various rhythms.

Section B: Use whole steps that are white to black or black to white; do not use pedal; involve various dynamics.

Section A: (return)

PERFORMANCE

1. Pay careful attention to dynamic markings.

Miniature March

LYNN FREEMAN OLSON

Teacher Accompaniment

2. Down stems in the student part are to be played with the left hand.

Alouette

French
Arranged by Lynn Freeman Olson

3. Perform as your teacher adds an accompaniment.

Waltz
from *The Merry Widow*

FRANZ LEHÁR
(1870–1948)
Arranged by Lynn Freeman Olson

4. Circle each shift of RH finger 2 before you play.

Hava Nagila

Israeli

* LH — down-stems

WRITING

1. Study the rhythm "shorthand" illustrated below.

Note	Shorthand	Drawn in pulse strokes	
♩	/	/	One stroke
♪ (half)	∠	∠	Two strokes
♩.	∠┘	∠┘	Three strokes
o	▱	▱	Four strokes
♫	⌐	⌐	Two quick strokes within one pulse

6-4 Several rhythm examples are played on the CD. Write each example using rhythmic shorthand in the space provided. Then convert each example to traditional notes. You will hear each example three times. Example 1 has been written in both rhythmic shorthand and traditional notation to show you how.

a.

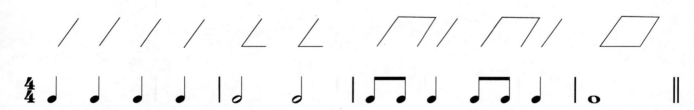

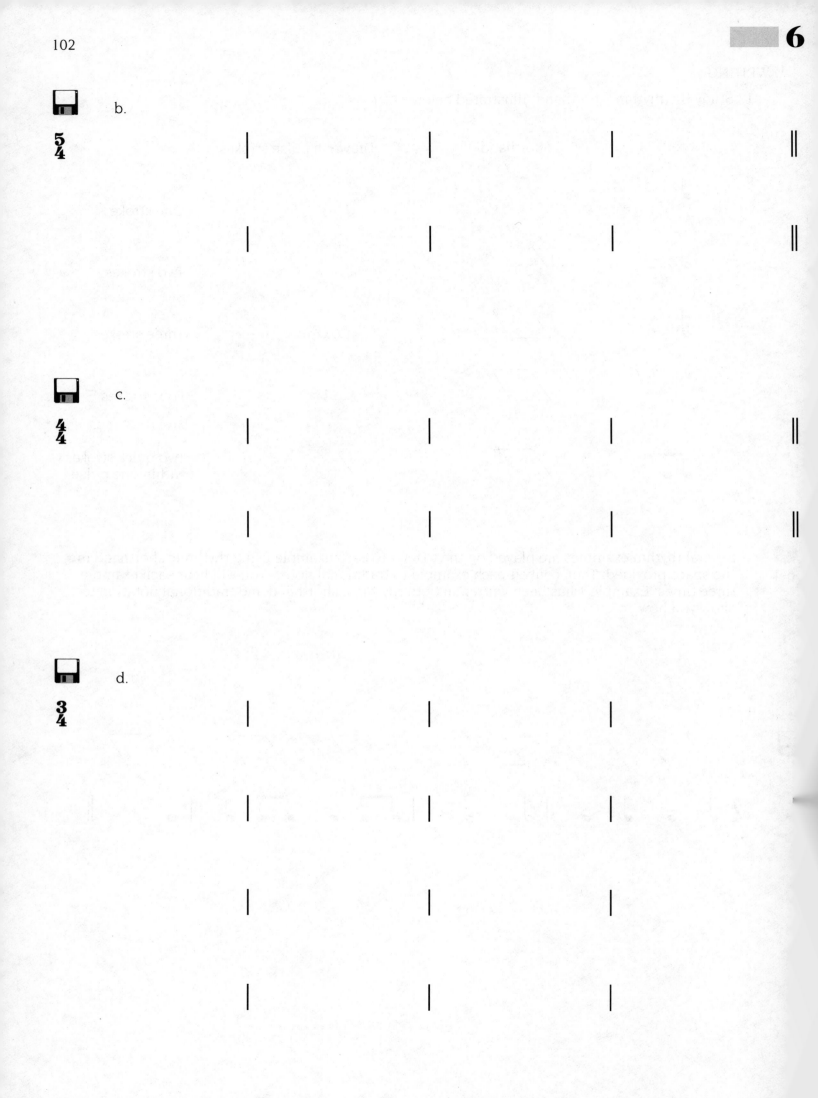

7.

Upbeats/Major Pentascales

LISTENING

1. Study the following musical excerpts carefully. Notice that Chopin uses two phrases, which are marked. In Türk's *Allegro non Tanto*, the phrases are not marked. Listen as your teacher plays each excerpt. Identify where the first phrase ends in *Allegro non Tanto*.

Prelude

FRÉDÉRIC CHOPIN, Op. 28, No. 6
(1810–1849)

Allegro non Tanto

DANIEL GOTTLOB TÜRK
(1756–1813)

2. You will hear several examples that include 4ths and 5ths. Close your book and listen as your teacher gives instructions for the playbacks.

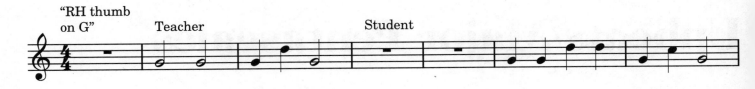

RHYTHM

> **Upbeat** One or more sounds preceding a downbeat (beginning of a measure). The last measure is usually shortened as a result.

1. Tap and count the following rhythm examples that begin with upbeats.

1   2   3 | 1   2   3

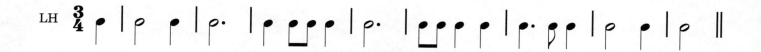

& 2 & | 1 & 2 &

2 3 4 | 1 & 2 & 3 & 4 &

2. In the $\frac{4}{4}$ rhythm chart, use the following physical motions for given note values:

♫ — CLAP

♩ — SNAP

♩ — TAP

Count aloud as you perform only the quarter notes.

Count aloud as your perform only the half notes.

Count aloud as your perform only the eighth notes.

Form a rhythm ensemble by assigning certain note values to certain students. When you perform together, you will hear all the rhythms given.

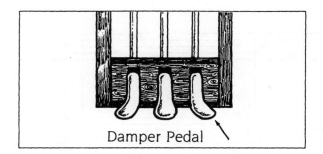

Damper Pedal

1. The following graphic shows the use of the pedal that sustains sounds (a *damper pedal* on acoustic pianos). It indicates foot action. Pedal with your heel on the floor; lower and raise the pedal with the ball of the foot. Use your right foot.

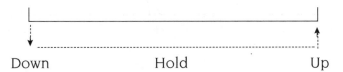

    Down   Hold   Up

    The graphic below shows connection of sounds. When the key or keys go down, the foot allows the pedal to rise to clear the previous sound and then lowers to catch the new sound. A seamless effect results.

    With finger 2, play the following and connect one tone to the next with the pedal as shown.

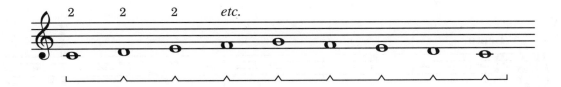

2. Play the following pedal exercises.

a.

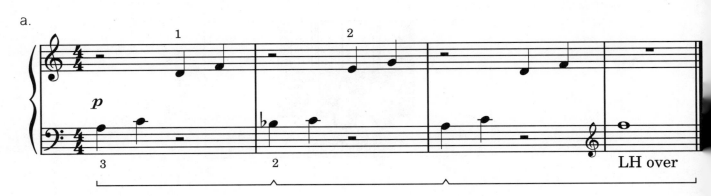

b.

c.

d. This is an alternate pedal designation.

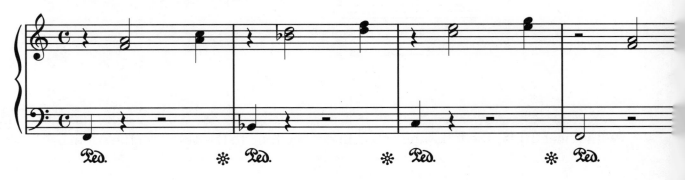

e.

<table>
<tr><td>**Staccato** Shortened sound
Legato Connected sound</td></tr>
</table>

> **Articulation** The manner in which notes are executed
>
> Staccato and legato are examples of articulation.

3. The Italian word *staccato* derives from a word meaning *to pull apart* or *detach*. In playing *staccato*, you do not punch the keys or jump away from them; you simply shorten each sound by releasing the key. You will feel your hand "release" easily. A dot above or below the notehead indicates *staccato*.

Play each example.

In playing *legato*, note durations are held for full value, resulting in continuous but not overlapping sound.

A special sign is not always necessary to show a legato sound.

4. Determine the range of each example to help in choice of fingering, then play.

a.

b.

c.

d.

Andante

e.

Sturdily

f.

Lively

THEORY

Scale   Individual pitches arranged in consecutive order

Pentascale   Five-tone scale using consecutive letter names

1. Beginning with RH finger 1, play an all white-key pentascale on G.

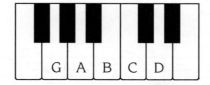

There are five pitches—1, 2, 3, 4, 5. The only half step occurs between which pitch numbers?

This is a MAJOR pentascale.

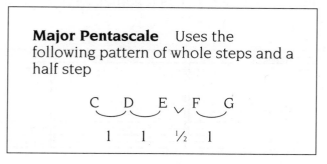

Major Pentascale Uses the following pattern of whole steps and a half step

Play and name major pentascales starting on C, D, E, F, G, and A, first RH and then LH. Which of these major pentascales uses a *flat*?

READING

1. *Reading flashes.* Prepare the position shown. During each measure of rest, your teacher will call the number of the next flash to be played. Reading will be nonstop from one to the other.

2. During the measure of rest, study each pair of notes, then play hands together. Keep a steady pulse throughout the exercise.

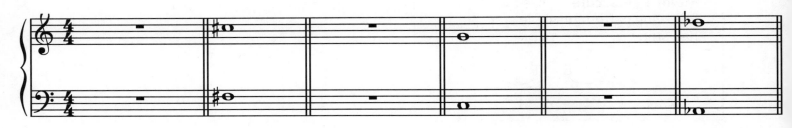

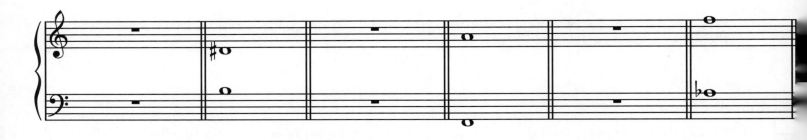

'Tis the Gift to Be Simple

3.

Shak
arr. Lynn Freeman Ols

4. Observe pedal markings.

IMPROVISATION

Take a Break

LYNN FREEMAN OLSON

PERFORMANCE

1. Pay close attention to alternating staccato and legato in *Dance*.

Dance

LYNN FREEMAN OLSON

2. Notice clef signs before playing.

Allegro

CORNELIUS GURLITT, Op. 117, No.
(1820–1901)

7

3. Perform as your teacher adds an accompaniment.

Amazing Grace

American
Arranged by Martha Hilley

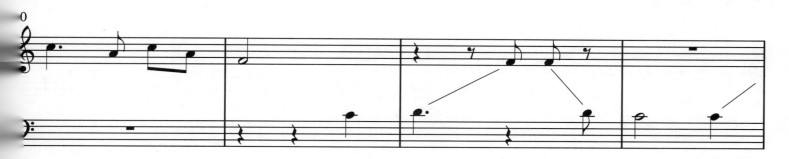

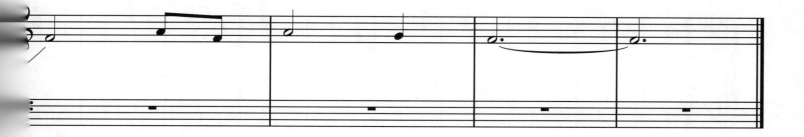

> ⅞ **Eighth Rest**   Equivalent to the
> eighth note in duration

7

4. The melody is divided between left and right hands. Determine the range of each before playing.
Note the use of an upbeat.

She'll Be Comin' Round the Mountain

American
Arranged by Martha Hilley

Teacher Accompaniment

5. Pay careful attention to the pedal indication. On which beat of the measure does it begin?

Song in the Alps

LYNN FREEMAN OLSON

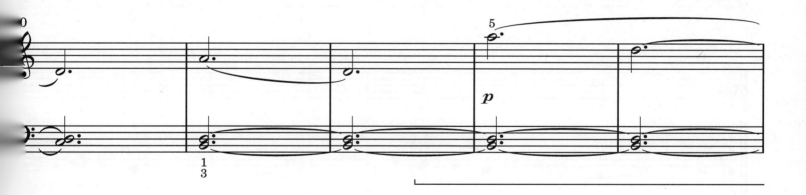

6. Play three times and move to the next part with each playing.

Our Song

LYNN FREEMAN OLSON

* Part 1 = Major pentascales, in direction and range shown:

WRITING

7-1

1. Four different rhythm examples are played on the CD or MIDI disk. Each example will be played three times. Write each one in the space below. Begin with light rhythm shorthand.

    a.

    b.

    c.

    d.

2. Each row represents a major pentascale. Fill in the blanks. Pentascales use consecutive letter names.

```
A    B    ___    ___    E

C    ___    ___    ___    G

D    ___    ___    G    ___

G    ___    ___    ___    ___

F    ___    A    ___    ___
```

124

8.

Recap

PERFORMANCE

1. Strive for a legato tone.

Aura Lee

American
Arranged by Lynn Freeman Olson

2. Perform twice, changing parts the second time around.

Lightly Row

Traditional
Arranged by Martha Hilley

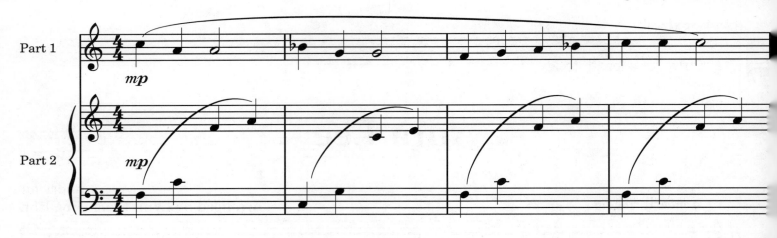

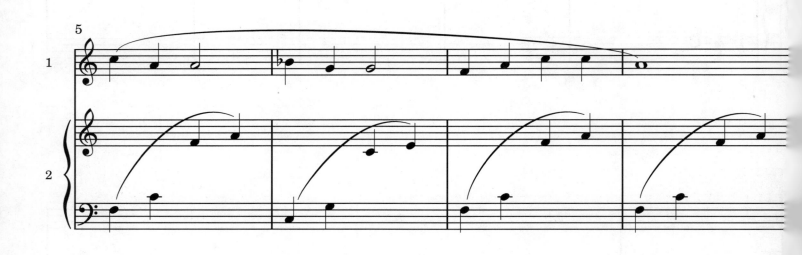

5. Use consecutive fingering for a connected left hand.

Danza

LYNN FREEMAN OLSON

6. Notice clef changes.

Melancholy

LYNN FREEMAN OLSON

TERMINOLOGY REVIEW

Discuss the following musical terms:

- Treble clef/bass clef
- Grand staff
- Interval
- Broken and blocked intervals
- *Andante/allegro/lento/vivace*
- Phrase/accent/slur
- Sharp/flat/natural
- Half step/whole step
- Scale/pentascale/major pentascale
- *mf* / *mp*
- Upbeat
- Repeat sign
- Enharmonic
- Staccato/legato
- Articulation
- Eighth rest

WRITING REVIEW

On the keyboard segment, write the letter names of the following major pentascales.

C

D

E

F

G

A

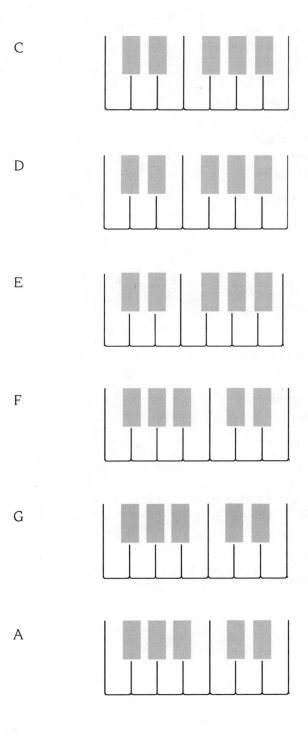

9.

Extensions/Triads/Leger Lines

LISTENING

ff *Fortissimo* Very loud	**Ritardando** *rit.* Gradual slowing
pp *Pianissimo* Very soft	of tempo
	Poco Little

Moderato   Moderate tempo
Allegretto   A little less *allegro*

1. Listen carefully as your teacher randomly plays portions of the following musical examples. Identify which are played. Can you identify examples of any of the boxed items above as your teacher plays?

Echoing

LOUIS KÖHLER
(1820–1886)

Rigaudon

ALEXANDER GOEDICKE
(1877–1957)

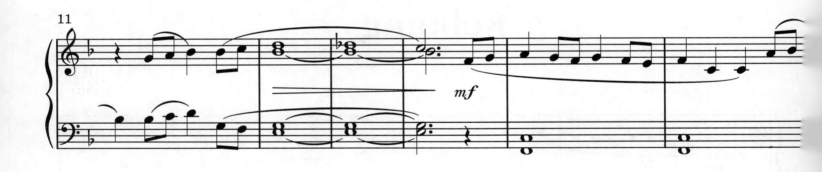

Quiet Conversation

LYNN FREEMAN OLSON

2. You will hear several examples based on pentascales. Close your book and listen as your teacher gives instructions for the playbacks.

"RH thumb on C"   Teacher   Student

"RH thumb on G"

"RH thumb on D"

Teacher may transpose to other keys.

RHYTHM

9-1   Tap the following two-handed rhythm exercises as the CD or MIDI disk provides a background. Use different surfaces for each hand.

1.

2.

3.

4.

5.

TECHNIQUE

1. Play the following pentascale pieces.

a.

b.

c.

d.
Sturdily

2. On a flat surface, play left-hand 5 4 3 2 1. Play again; this time "roll" on the corner of your thumb so that the other fingers move as a unit slightly to the right:

     5   4   3   2   ①
                               roll

When you roll, your fourth finger will be in line with your thumb:

Begin: 5 4 3 2 ①
                        (5 4 3)

Roll back: 5 4 3 2 ①

Now play a major pentascale on the keyboard. When you cross, your third finger will play a whole step above the pattern.

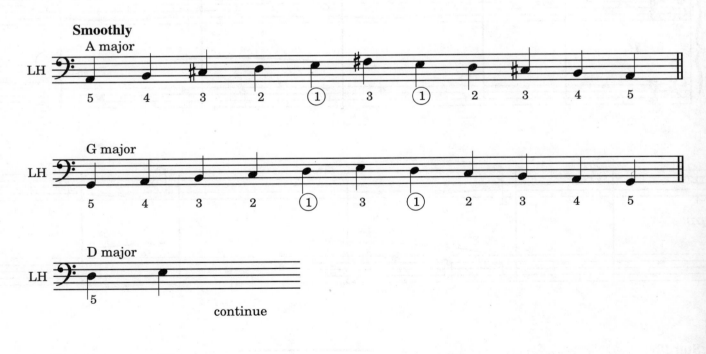

Smoothly
A major

LH   5   4   3   2   ①   3   ①   2   3   4   5

G major

LH   5   4   3   2   ①   3   ①   2   3   4   5

D major

LH   5

continue

C major

LH   5

continue

Practice a right-hand crossing by rolling on your thumb. Play a major pentascale upward and downward. When you return to the thumb, roll as you did with the left hand, but play a half step below with finger 2.

Play also in D, E, F, G, and A major.

3. Study the following locations. Then play each example with the single hand indicated.

a. Note the rests!

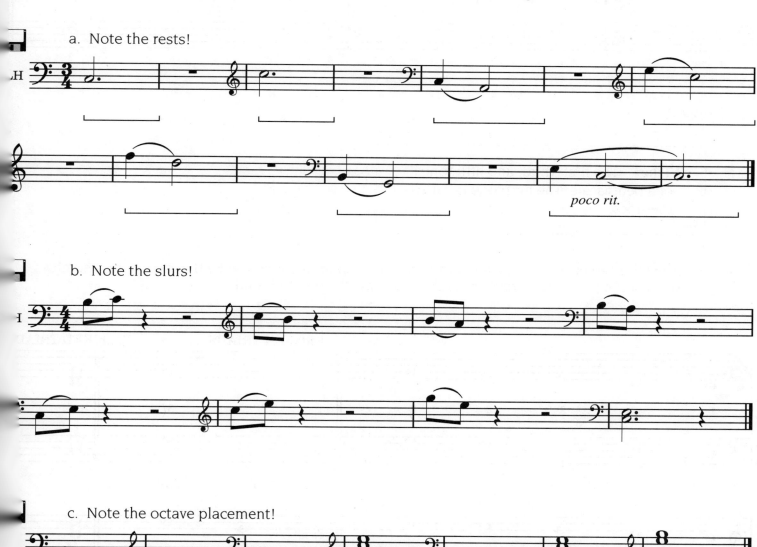

b. Note the slurs!

c. Note the octave placement!

4. Pay close attention to clef changes and octave placement.

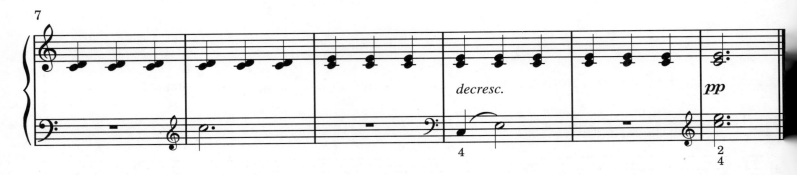

THEORY

> **Triad** The first, third, and fifth tones of a pentascale. The first tone is called the "root."

1. Study the two examples shown below. Play the pentascale followed by the root, third, and fifth tones of the pentascale (broken triad). Then play the blocked triad.

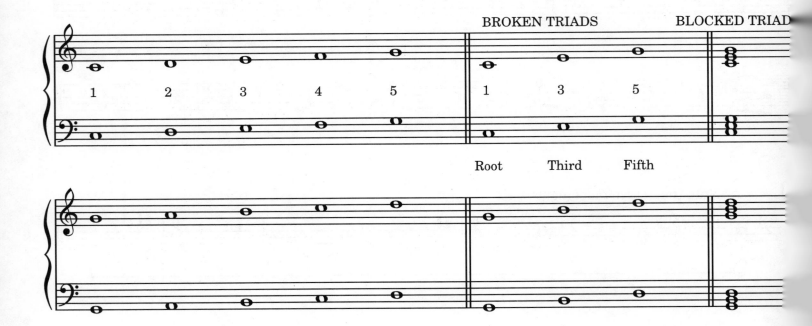

Complete the following examples in the same manner

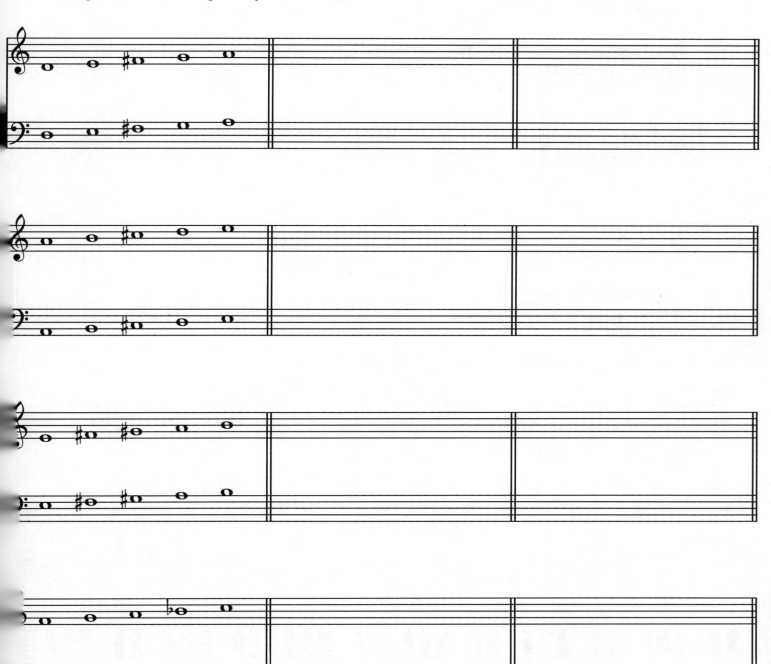

Now play the pentascale/triad exercise in all six keys nonstop. Your teacher will determine the order.

2. Play right-hand triads and left-hand root tones for all six keys. C is given as an example. Your teacher will determine the order.

READING

> **Leger Lines**   Used to indicate pitches above or below the five lines of the staff

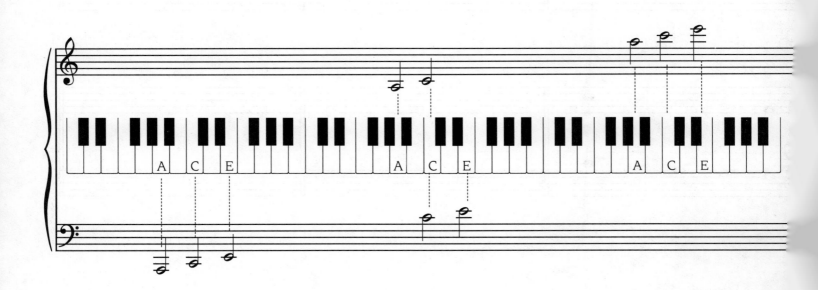

1. During the open measures, locate the next position. Look for triad and pentascale shapes. Play.

2. Play as written.

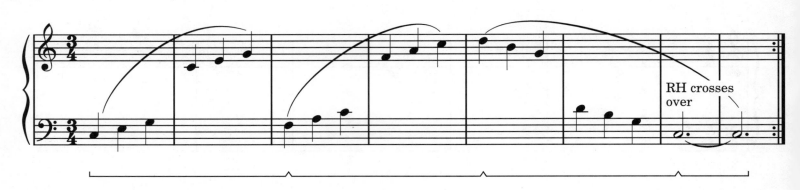

3. For each of the following, circle another group of notes identical in sound to the circled group; then play each example in its entirety after determining fingering.

a.

b.

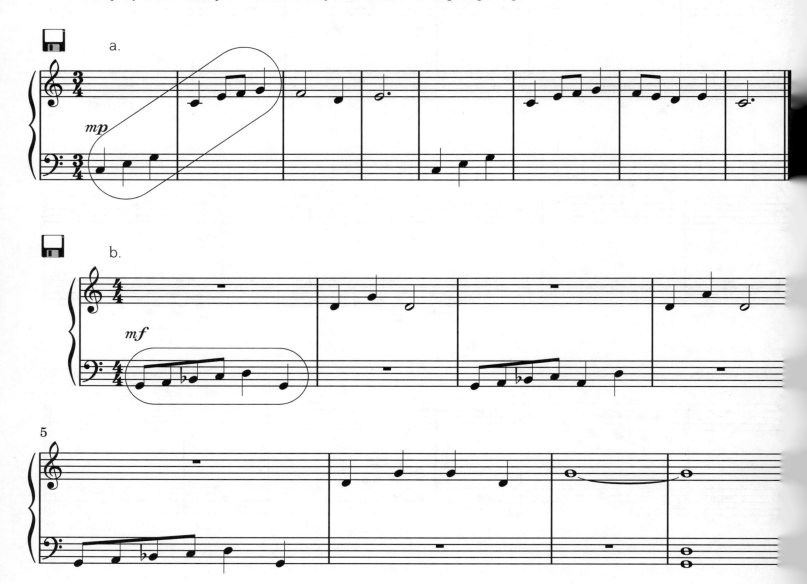

9

IMPROVISING

1. Improvise on triad tones with the right hand.

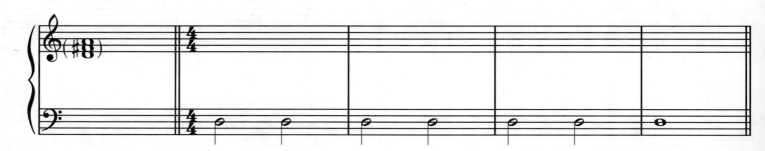

2. Your teacher will demonstrate different two-measure rhythms. Echo the rhythm by playing various tones of a pentascale. The pentascale will be determined by your teacher. Your final bar of improvisation should come to rest on the lowest tone of the pentascale. Close your book!

Teacher (clap or tap)   Student (play)

Lady Moon

LYNN FREEMAN OLSON

Hickory Breeze

LYNN FREEMAN OLSON

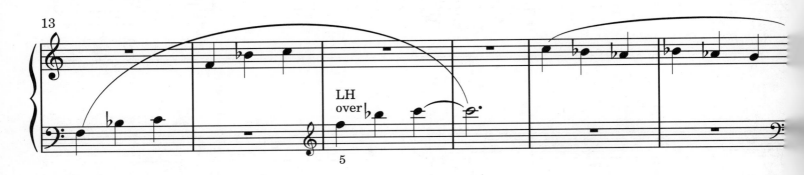

Echoing
(See page 135)

I Know Where I'm Going

Irish
Arranged by Martha Hilley

Ancient Temple

LYNN FREEMAN OLSON

Serenely flowing (in 2)

WRITING

1. Write triads on each staff using the first, third, and fifth tones of the indicated major pentascale.

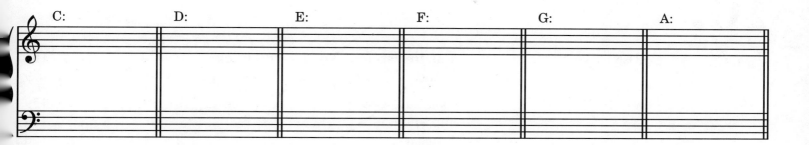

2. Compose a melody to go with the following ostinato. Play hands together.

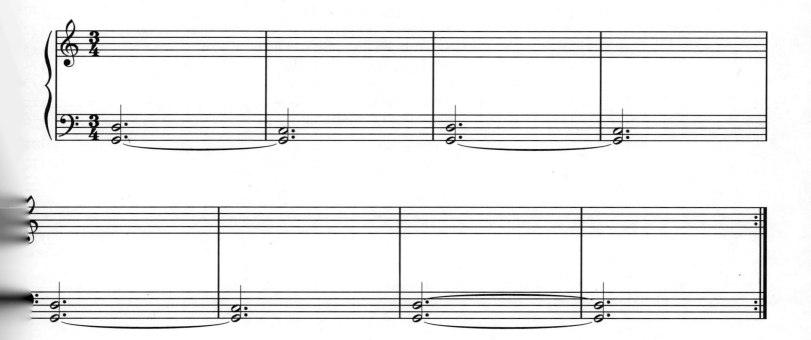

10.

Syncopation/Sixths, Sevenths, Eighths/Major Scales/Key Signatures

LISTENING

1. Locate the indicated keyboard position. Your teacher will play two-measure phrases, each beginning on D; there will be three beats to each measure. After your teacher has played the first two measures, sing back the phrase (use "la" or "loo," etc.). Your teacher will play the first two measures once again; now play these two measures on the keyboard. The same procedure will follow throughout the piece. Close your book!

Ear Investment No. 1

WOODY BUDNICK

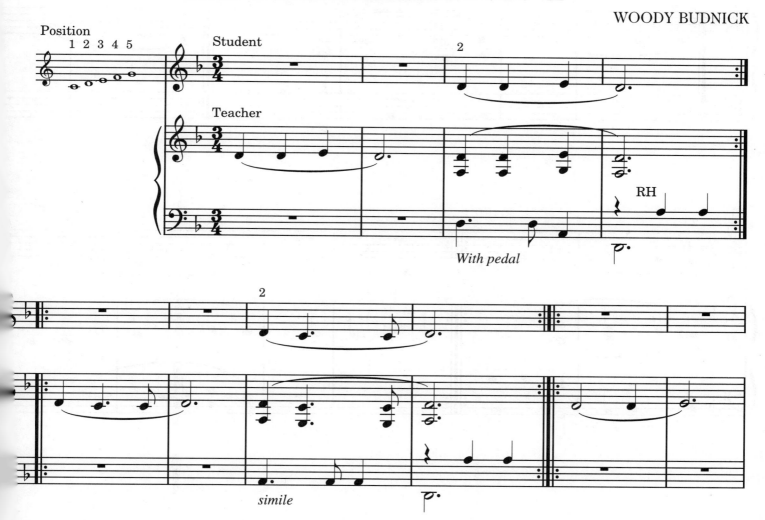

Reprinted by permission of the composer.

2. Listen as your teacher plays melodic half steps and whole steps. Identify each example as a half step or a whole step. If it sounds like the beginning of a major pentascale, it is a whole step; if it sounds smaller, it is a half step. Close your book!

RHYTHM

Syncopation   An emphasis on offbeats or weak beats

---

1. Tap and count aloud the following syncopated rhythm examples.

> ⌢ **Fermata**   Hold longer than the note value

2. Tap these rhythms that use a *fermata*.

TECHNIQUE

1. You can extend the pentascale beyond the five-note range in two ways:

   By moving your thumb away from your hand:

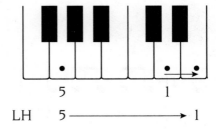

LH   5 ⟶ 1

By moving your hand away from your thumb:

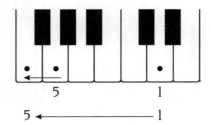

With each hand, practice extending the following pentascale positions two ways:

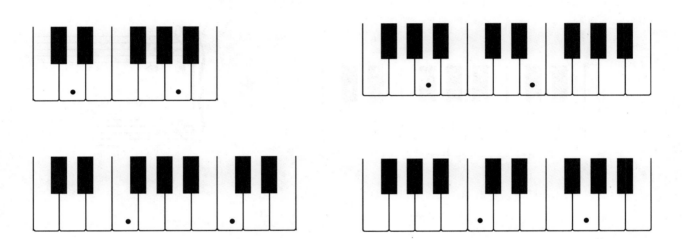

THEORY

1. From C to A is an interval of a sixth. Why?

C D E F G A

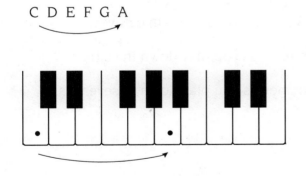

From C to B is an interval of a seventh. Why?

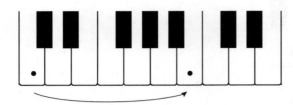 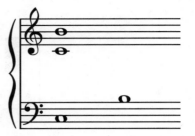

From C to C is an interval of an eighth (octave). Why?

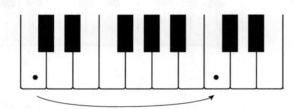 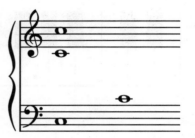

Play and say the following interval drills:

- Begin with the lowest A on your keyboard and say letter names as you play up in sixths.

- Begin with the lowest B and say letter names as you play up in sevenths.

- Begin with the lowest C and say letter names as you play up in octaves.

- Begin with the highest C and say letter names as you play down in sixths.

- Begin with the highest B and say letter names as you play down in sevenths.

2. A *major key* uses the tones of the major pentascale plus two additional tones.

Legato

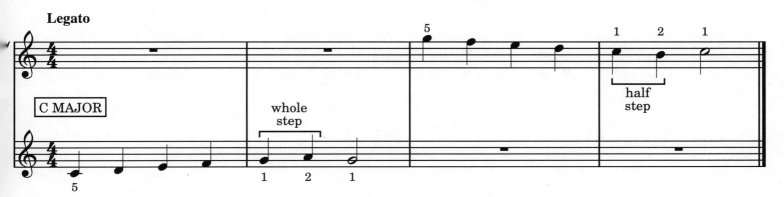

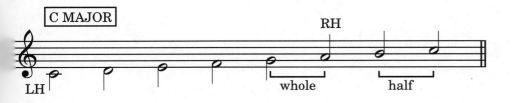

> **Key** A group of related tones named for their home tone (keynote, or tonic)
>
> **Leading tone** The tone that just precedes the tonic

A major scale can be built beginning on any white or black key. For now we will focus on six scales beginning on white keys. Above, you played all tones in the key of C major. No black keys were used. The complete C major scale looks like this:

This is the pattern of the whole steps and half steps for all major scales.

Play the two-handed exercises on each of the following keys; then write the scale. Why will the black keys always be *sharps*?

G   D   A   E

F major uses a flat.

The sharps or flats used in each scale may be shown on the staff in a traditional order.

Key Signature   A list of the sharps or flats used in a key

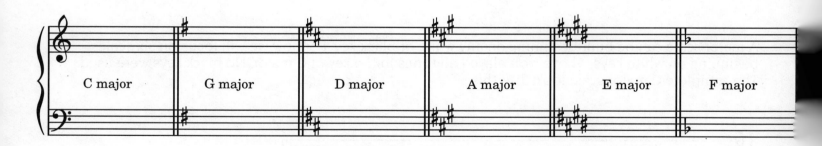

C major   G major   D major   A major   E major   F major

3. Play *Jingle Bells* with left-hand major triads. Note the use of a key signature.

Jingle Bells

JAMES PIERPONT
(1822–1893)

READING

1. The key signature influences notes of the same name, no matter where they appear. Before playing, notice all notes that will be sharped or flatted.

a.

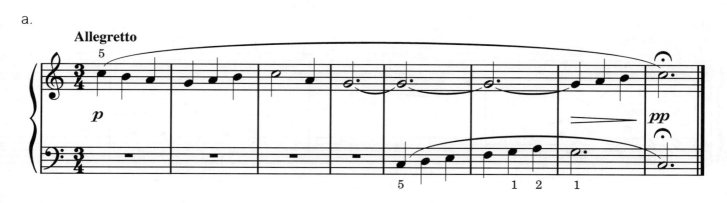

b. Circle the pitches affected by the key signature.

10

2. Scan the range of each group; plan fingering; play. Use the right hand in the treble staff and the left hand in the bass staff.

3. Plan for hand shifts in the left hand and expansions in the right hand. What triads are outlined in the left hand in bars 6 and 7? Study the leger lines carefully.

Caroline's Lullaby

MARTHA HILLE

4. Discover extensions before playing.

This Old Man

Traditional
Arranged by Martha Hilley

IMPROVISING

The "blues pentascale" alters a major pentascale:

1 — (omit 2) — ♭3 — 4 — ♭5 — ♮5

Play the blues pentascales on C, F, and G.

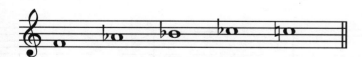

Improvise a melody using the C blues pentascale as your teacher provides a background (shown on next page).

 *Teacher Background*

PERFORMANCE

1. Pay close attention to octave placement.

Moonlight on the Water

LYNN FREEMAN OLSON

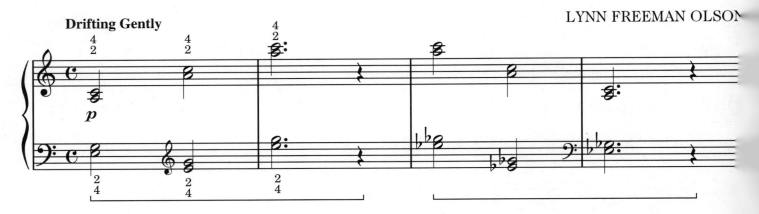

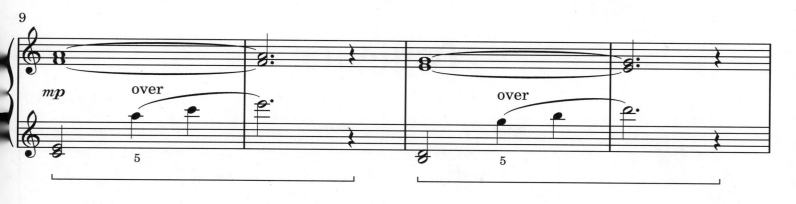

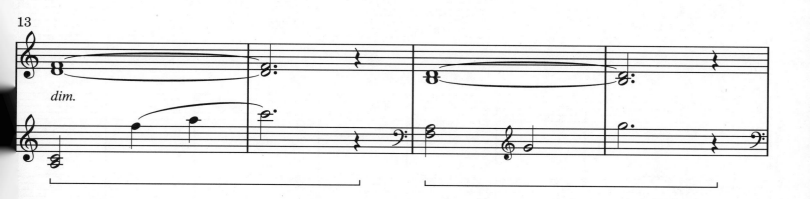

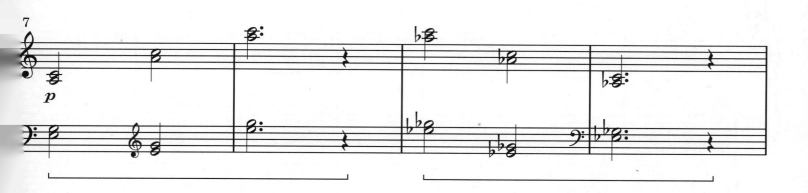

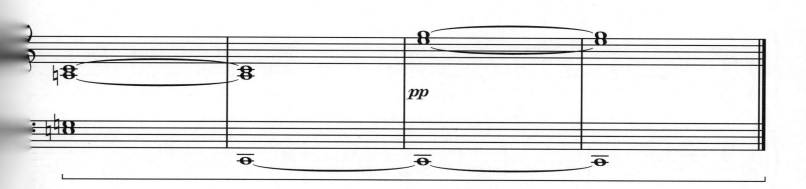

2.

Twilight

LYNN FREEMAN OLSON

| **Da Capo** From the beginning | **D.C. al Fine** Return to the beginning and play to the end |
| **Fine** The end | |

5.

Kum-Bah-Yah

African
Arranged by Lynn Freeman Olson

6.

Etude in G

LOUIS KÖHLER
(1820–1886)

WRITING

1. Circle any notes that would be sharps or flats. (Do not play.)

2. Copy each of the given clefs and key signatures. Name the major key.

11.

Scale Fingering/Primary Chords/Harmonizing/ Transposing

LISTENING

Pesante	Heavily
Leggiero	Lightly
Cantabile	Singing
Marcato	With marked emphasis
Andantino	A little faster than Andante
Scherzando	Playfully

1-1

1. Listen carefully to the six musical examples on the CD or MIDI disk. Determine which example is played *pesante*, which is played *leggiero*, which is played *cantabile*, which is played *marcato*, which is played *andantino*, and which is played *scherzando*.

RHYTHM

Select sounds. Consider clapping, tapping, knocking wood, striking metal, etc.

Fly Away

LYNN FREEMAN OLSON

TECHNIQUE

1. Practice this traditional right-hand fingering for the C major scale, two octaves.

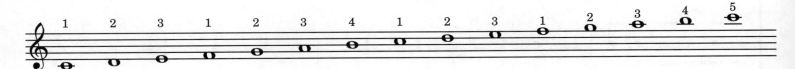

Now look carefully at this traditional left-hand fingering for the C major scale.

The fingering shown above is used for the following major scales: C D E G A.

Play each of the scales, hands separately, two octaves up and back down.

2. Play the following melodic and harmonic interval exercises.

a.

b.

c.

3. During each rest, prepare the next blocked interval with the hand away from the keyboard.

4. Play these technique studies; keep your hand relaxed.

a.

b.

c.

d.

e.

f.

Tonic	Home tone or keynote
Dominant	Fifth tone of a scale
Subdominant	Fourth tone of scale

1. In a major pentascale, the bottom tone is called tonic (I) and the top tone is called dominant (V). The subdominant (IV) is the fourth tone.

Generally, when a melody is made mostly of tones 1, 3, and 5, you would accompany with tonic (I); when the melody is mostly 2 and 4, you would accompany with dominant (V); when the melody centers on 4 alone, you have the option of dominant (V) or subdominant (IV). Your ear will always be the final test of appropriate accompaniment.

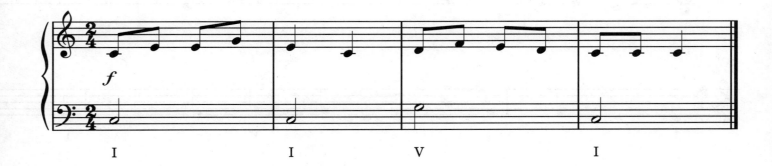

To accompany right-hand melodies, you may choose to use the left-hand pentascale position as illustrated. We also encourage the frequent use of dominant and subdominant *below* tonic. This is easy when you place your left-hand thumb on a white-key tonic.

2. Accompany the following melodies with tonic, dominant, and subdominant tones. Try both "dominant/ subdominant above" and "dominant/subdominant below" left-hand positions.

3. Tonic (I), dominant (V), and subdominant (IV) triads are built on the first, fifth, and fourth tones of the scale. Play the following exercises using I, V, and IV triads. Spell the next triad aloud during each measure of rest.

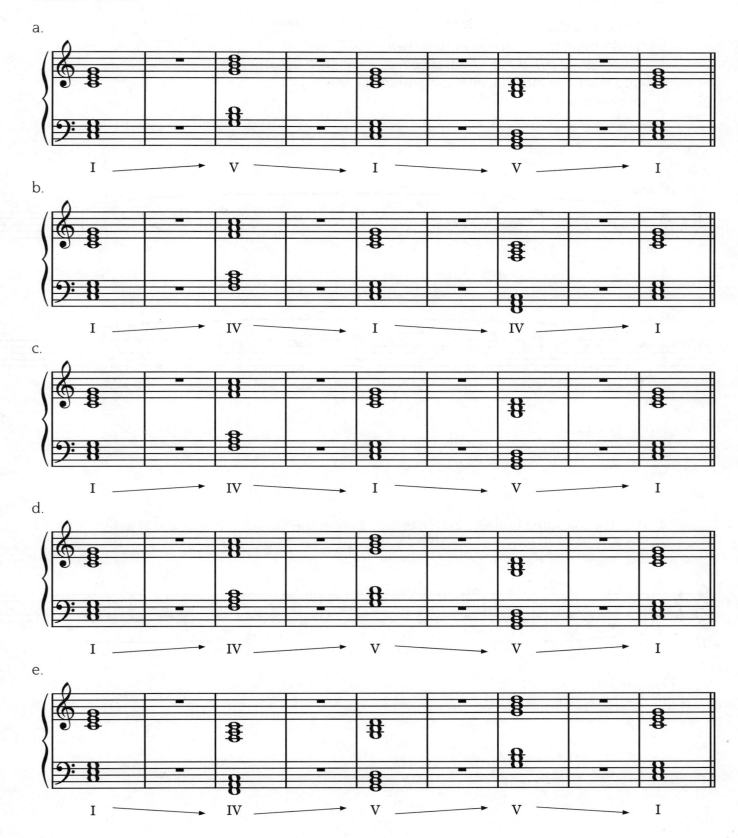

a.

I ⟶ V ⟶ I ⟶ V ⟶ I

b.

I ⟶ IV ⟶ I ⟶ IV ⟶ I

c.

I ⟶ IV ⟶ I ⟶ V ⟶ I

d.

I ⟶ IV ⟶ V ⟶ V ⟶ I

e.

I ⟶ IV ⟶ V ⟶ V ⟶ I

Play the harmonic patterns again using these major keys: D E F G A.

> **Transposition**   Writing and/or
> performing music in a key other than
> the original key. When you transpose,
> you think the melodic intervals within
> the new key.

F major

G major

4. Play the following C major exercise; then play in the keys of G major and D major.

Bounce

LYNN FREEMAN OLSON

Southern Tune

American
Arranged by Lynn Freeman Olson

IMPROVISING

1. The right-hand melody of the following piece uses the C blues pentascale. The left-hand plays single-tone roots of the harmony shown by Roman numerals. Play as written.

C blues pentascale

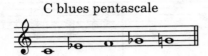

Easily

Play again, this time varying the right-hand rhythm. For example:

etc.

Listen to the MIDI disk performance of a "varied" rhythm.

2. Follow the chord changes below. The left hand plays single-tone roots; the right hand improvises using the G blues pentascale (the pentascale never has to change position).

Key of G

$\frac{4}{4}$	I	IV	I	I
	IV	IV	I	I
	V	IV	I	I*

*Notice that the piece and the chart follow the same pattern of single-tone roots.

3.

Noon Clouds

LYNN FREEMAN OLSON

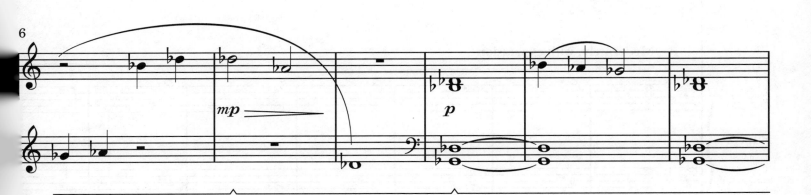

4.

Sugarloaf Mountain

EVERETT STEVE

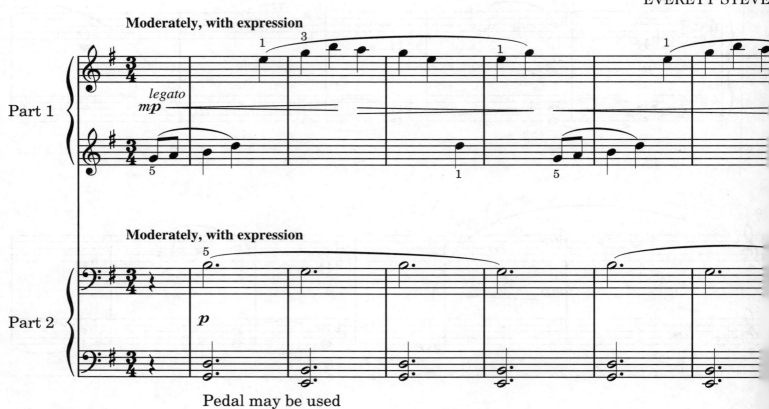

Pedal may be used

11

A Little Joke
from *24 Pieces for Children*

DMITRI KABALEVSKY, Op. 39, No. 6
(1904–1987)

* A short line (–) by a notehead indicates emphasis by sustaining. In this case, it makes the *staccato* a bit less short. The Italian word for this sign is *tenuto*.

WRITING

1. Write triads for the following major keys. Use necessary sharps or flats with the triads (rather than signatures).

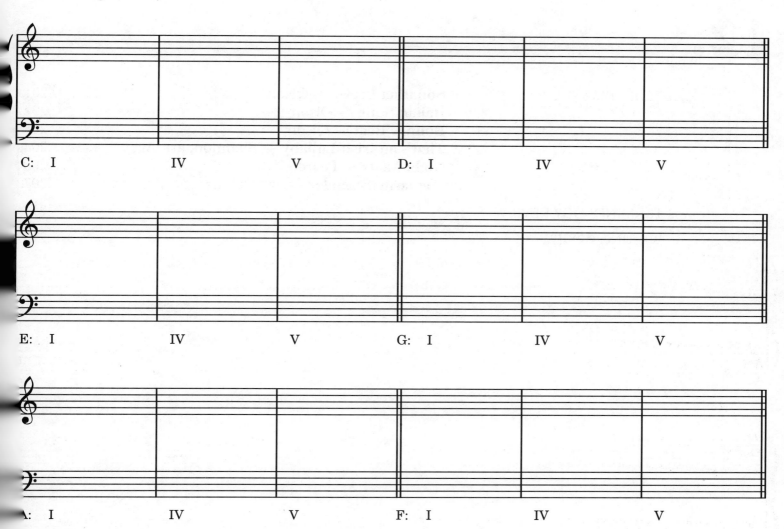

2. Rewrite this melody in D major and C major.

12.

Recap

PERFORMANCE

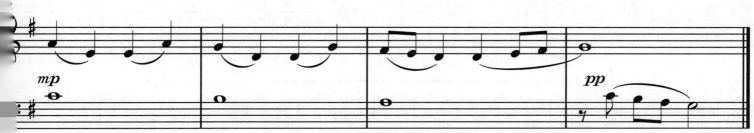 1. Supply fingerings before playing.

Sonatina Breve

LYNN FREEMAN OLSON

Italian Song

LYNN FREEMAN OLSON

2.

Allegretto, cantabile

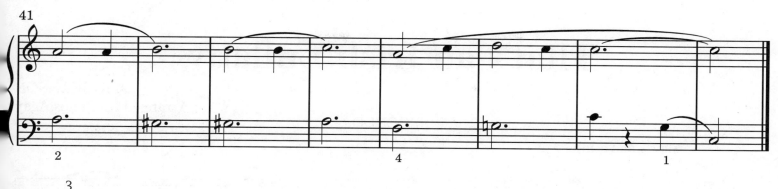

Bounce Beat

LYNN FREEMAN OLSON

4.

That's an Irish Lullaby

J. R. SHANNON
Arranged by Denes Agay

SECONDO

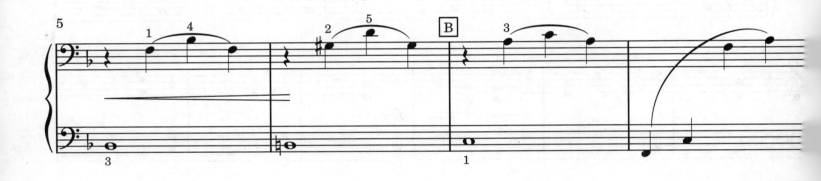

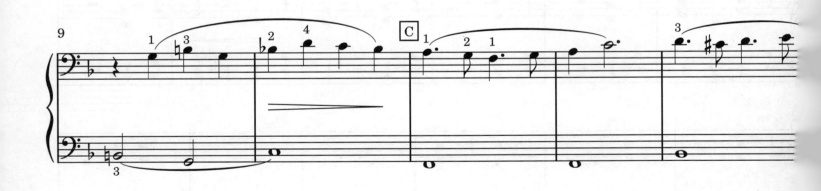

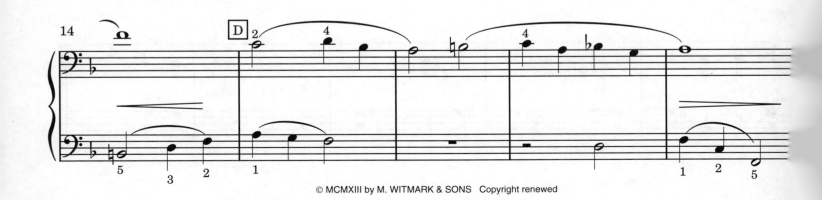

That's an Irish Lullaby

J. R. SHANNON
Arranged by Denes Agay

PRIMO

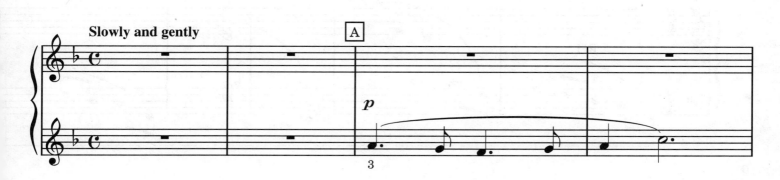

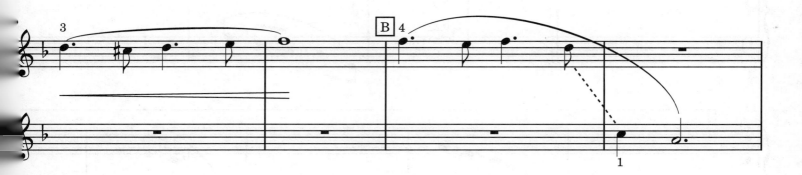

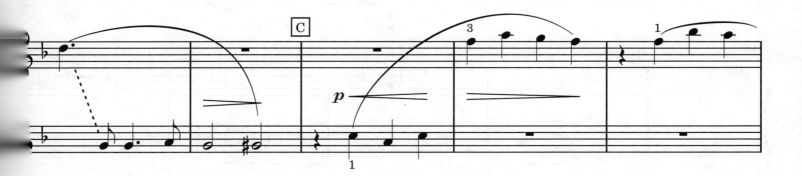

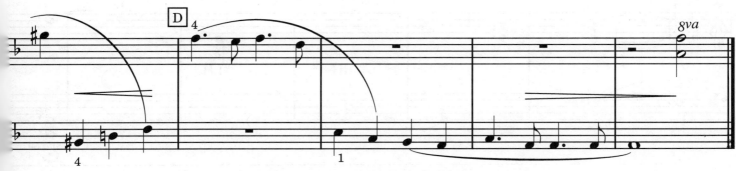

5.

Night Mists

ELVINA TRUMAN PEARCE

Wayfarin' Stranger

Arranged by Ann Collins

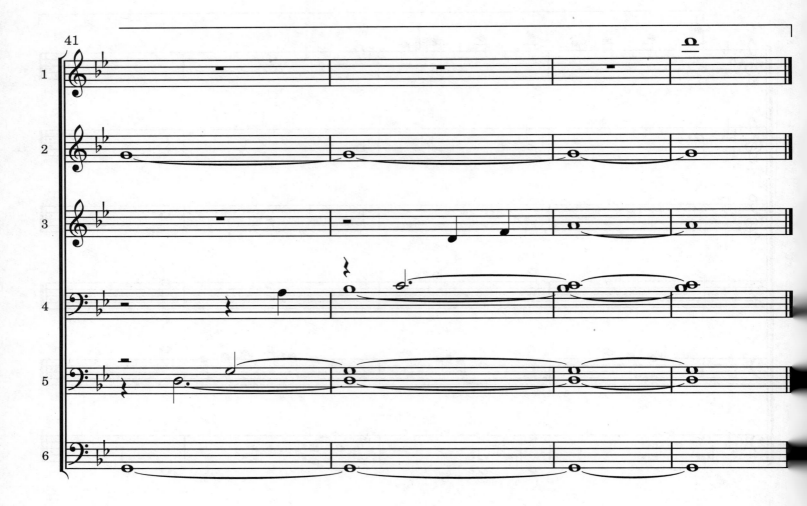

TERMINOLOGY REVIEW

Discuss the following musical terms:

- Triad/root, third, fifth
- Leger lines
- Syncopation
- Fermata
- Sixths/sevenths/octaves
- Key/key signature
- Leading tone
- Tonic/dominant/subdominant

- Pesante/leggiero/cantabile/marcato/Andantino/scherzando
- *ff* / *pp*
- Transposition
- Moderato/allegretto
- Ritardando
- Poco
- D.C. al Fine

WRITING REVIEW

1. Complete the following interval chains by writing the note-name answer.

B,   up a 4th   F,   down a 2nd
     down a 6th   up a 5th
     up a 3rd   down a 6th
     down a 7th   up a 7th

     _____   _____

D,   up a 4th   E,   down a 4th
     down a 5th   up a 3rd
     up a 6th   down a 7th
     down a 7th   up a 6th

     _____   _____

2. Write these major scales on the keyboards below.

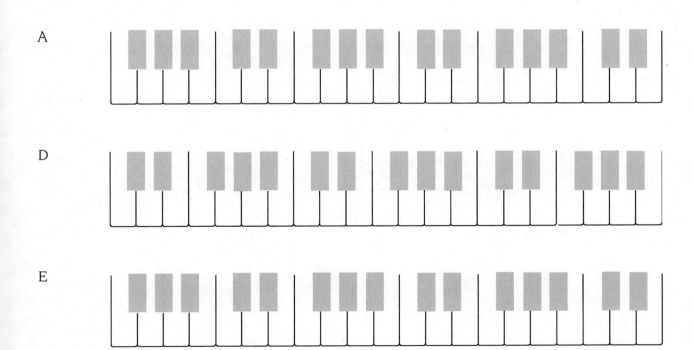

A

D

E

13.

13

Chord Inversions/ Guitar Symbols

LISTENING

> **Accelerando** *accel.* Becoming faster
>
> **A tempo** To return to the original or previous tempo after such indications as *rit.* or *accel.*

3-1

1. Listen carefully to the three musical examples on the CD or MIDI disk. As the examples are replayed, determine which examples use *rit.*, *accel.*, and/or *a tempo*.

2. Find the first three keys of the D major pentascale in your right hand. Your teacher will play four-measure phrases using these pitches. Play back after each four-measure phrase. Close your book!

Ear Investment No. 2

WOODY BUDNICK

Reprinted by permission of the composer.

RHYTHM

1. Tap the following rhythms that use an eighth-note upbeat and an eighth rest.

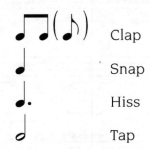

2. Use the following sounds in the ⁴⁄₄ rhythm chart:

    Clap

    Snap

    Hiss

    Tap

Form a rhythm ensemble and perform.

TECHNIQUE

1. Notice chord shapes as you play these exercises.

a.

b.

c.

d.

e.

f.

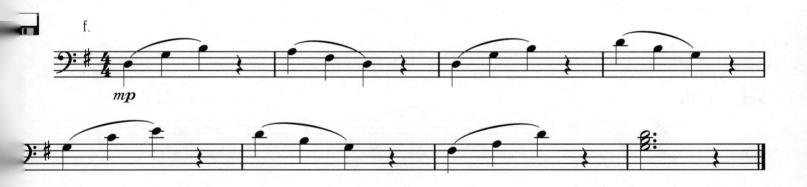

2. Review the following scales, hands separately, as the CD or MIDI disk provides a rhythmic background:

    C   D   E   G   A

Play the scales once more, this time hands together in *contrary* motion. Use the following example as a guide.

3. The following phrases use finger crossings. For each, plan a logical fingering that involves a crossing.

a.

b.

c.

d.

e.

4. The following exercises involve wide leaps. To move, look quickly at the keyboard when necessary and, just as quickly, focus again on the printed page.

a.

b.

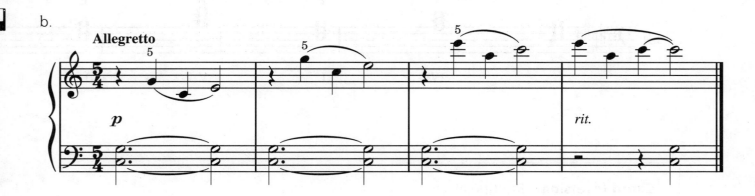

c.

d.

THEORY

1. Chords may be designated in different ways—by Roman numeral as shown in Chapter 11 (I, IV, V) or by letter name (usually called guitar symbols). Most popular music will have guitar symbols written above the vocal line. These symbols represent the harmonies that have been used in that particular arrangement.

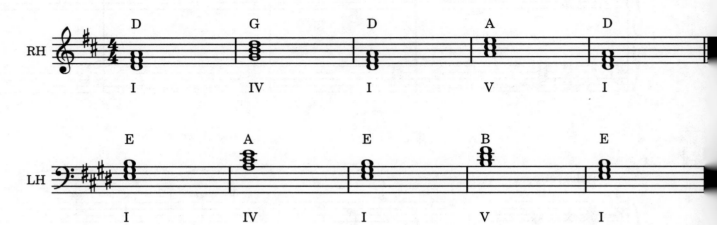

Chord Inversion	Root position rearranged

2. Inverted chords provide economy of motion when moving from one chord to the next. Play through the following "closest possible position" chord exercise.

The shape of inverted chords is designated by figures (Arabic numerals):

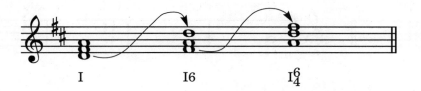

Arrows point to pitches
rearranged from triad to triad.

or by letter name:

The letter name following the slash
mark (/) will always indicate the
lowest sounding pitch.

Chord designations in *Piano for Pleasure* will be primarily guitar symbols.

3. "Closest possible position" chords share common tones in many instances. Mark the *common tones* in the examples shown below by drawing a line between them. Refer to item 2 if needed.

Play the following root position triads followed by their inversions.

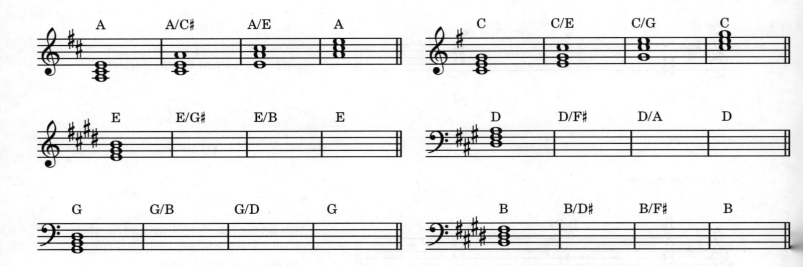

Assign the proper Roman numeral to each root position triad used above.

4. Return to the single-tone harmonization in Chapter 11 (p. 186) and play again using triads in the closest position possible. Think guitar symbols.

READING

1. When reading chords, notice the interval formed by the two "outside" notes; then mentally fill in the other note or notes.

For example:

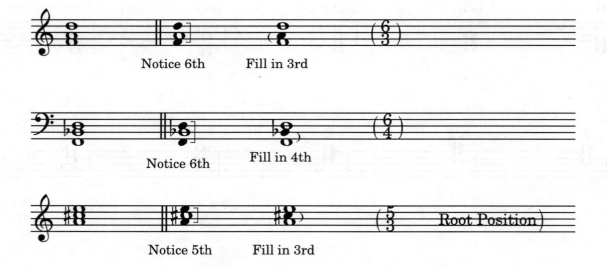

Notice 6th   Fill in 3rd

Notice 6th   Fill in 4th

Notice 5th   Fill in 3rd

Use the preceding reading method and play the following exercise.

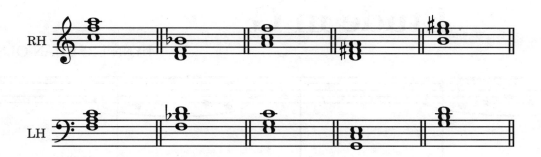

2. Look for "common tones" in the right-hand accompaniment.

Study in G

LUDVIG SCHYTTE, Op. 108, No. 12
(1848–1909)

3. Pay close attention to indicated articulations.

Etude in G

LYNN FREEMAN OLSON

LH over RH

IMPROVISING

1. Return to *Wayfarin' Stranger* (p. 207). Divide the class on parts 3, 4, 5, and 6. These parts can accompany melodic improvisation based on the following ideas.

Or you might use some combination of these ideas.

(The balance of this page has been left blank to eliminate a difficult page turn.)

PERFORMANCE

1. Note the use of syncopation.

Left's Turn Only

(Left-Hand Solo)

ROBERT VANDALL

Emotions

JOSEPH M. MARTIN

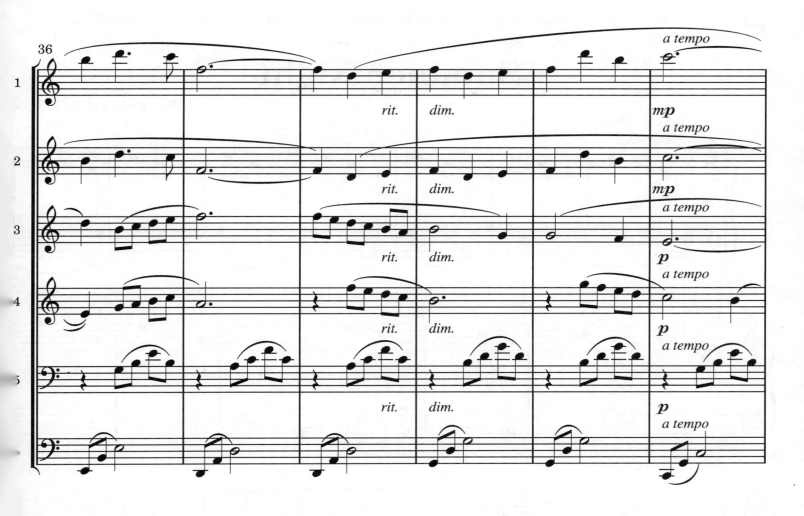

 **13**

3. The first sixteen measures and the last twelve measures use *no* pedal. Your fingers should do the work!

Summer Night

LYNN FREEMAN OLSON

4. Note chord shapes and clef changes.

Lingering Essence

JEANINE YEAGER

5.

Triadique

LYNN FREEMAN OLSON

*Prestissimo means very fast.

WRITING

1. Furnish the following chords using the principle of closest possible position. Indicate the inversion used. The first exercise gives an example.

a.

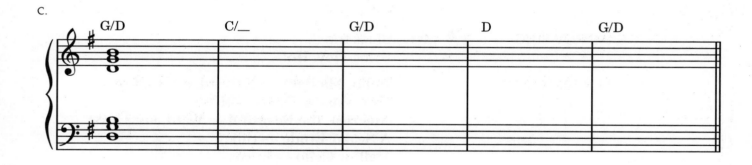

b.

c.

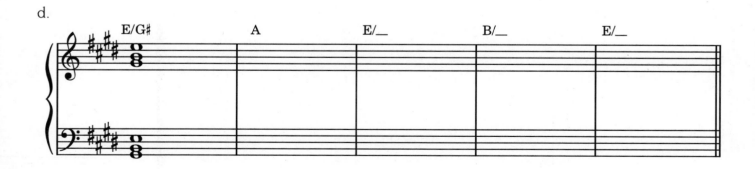

d.

14.

Sixteenth Notes/Interval Quality/Dominant Sevenths

LISTENING

14-1

1. Listen carefully to the several rhythm examples on the CD or MIDI disk. Tap back after each example.

2. Your teacher will play randomly from the following examples. Be prepared to identify which example is being performed.

a.

b.

c.

d.

e.

f.

RHYTHM

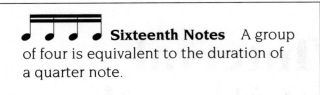

Sixteenth Notes A group of four is equivalent to the duration of a quarter note.

1. Tap the following rhythms using sixteenth notes.

2. Chant and tap the following folk lyric.

Hey, Ho!

English

Next, tap and chant as a group in a rhythm round. Divide into four parts. When part 1 reaches *, part 2 starts at the beginning. When part 1 reaches **, part 3 starts at the beginning. When part 1 reaches ***, part 4 begins.

Continue until each part has completed the lyric twice. Part 4 will finish alone. Each part should tap a different sounding surface (part 1—piano top, part 2—bench, etc.).

TECHNIQUE

1. Play these examples that use broken triads.

a.

b.

senza pedal*

c.

Senza means "without."

2. Play this crossing study until finger shifts come naturally. Then repeat the exercise in the keys of C, E, G, and A.

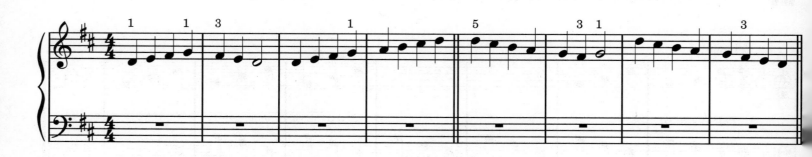

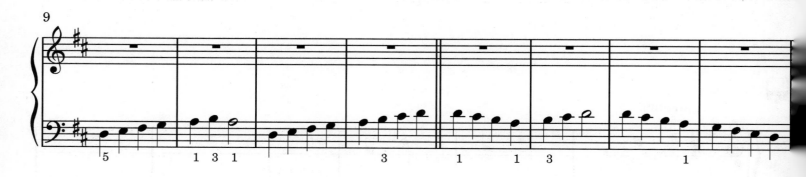

3. Study the following fingering for scales, hands together, two octaves. Practice the fingering on a flat surface several times before using it to play the following major scales.

	C		D	E		G	A							
RH	1	2	③	1	2	③	4	1	2	③	1	2	③	4	5
LH	5	4	③	2	1	③	2	1	4	③	2	1	③	2	1

THEORY

1. Intervals in music have further qualities than their distance designation. They may be called major, minor, diminished, or augmented. This is determined by the *number* of whole steps and half steps used to build the particular interval.

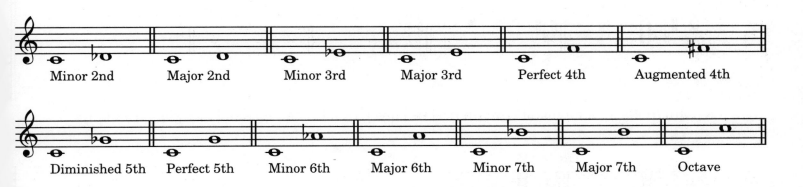

Minor 2nd   Major 2nd   Minor 3rd   Major 3rd   Perfect 4th   Augmented 4th

Diminished 5th   Perfect 5th   Minor 6th   Major 6th   Minor 7th   Major 7th   Octave

2. Study the triads below and determine the quality of the intervals used.

Example:

Major triad   Minor triad   Diminished triad   Augmented triad

Dominant Seventh   Chord built on fifth degree of the scale. It consists of the dominant triad plus a minor seventh above the root.

3. Study the intervals marked in each dominant seventh.

Key of C

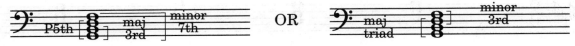

4. For *each major key shown*, play a dominant seventh in the right hand. Think: tonic, dominant, dominant seventh.

Example:

As with triads, the dominant seventh may be shown by a Roman numeral or a guitar symbol.

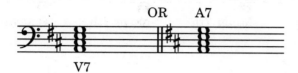

C7 The letter by itself stands for a major triad; the 7, when used with a letter, stands for a minor seventh.	**V7** The seventh can be major or minor; it is determined by the key signature. In a V7, the seventh is always minor.

5. When playing the following progressions, verbally spell each chord in root position but play the closest position (as written). Think about the pitches that stay the same from chord to chord (common tones). Don't move your whole hand away from the keys if you have common tones.

a.

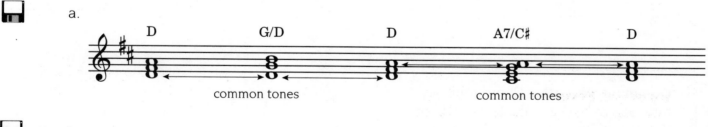

b.

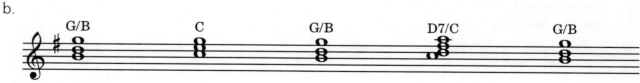

c.

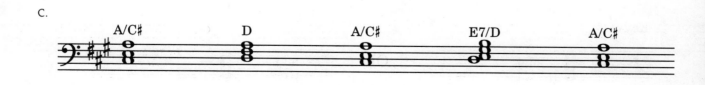

d.

e.

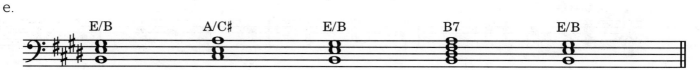

6. Review the pattern for major scales.

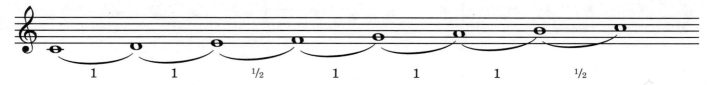

Build major scales on each of the following pitches.

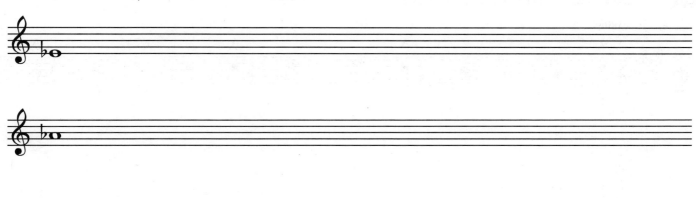

7. As with sharps, the flats in a key signature occur in a traditional order. Study each of the following major key signatures carefully and then copy each in the space provided.

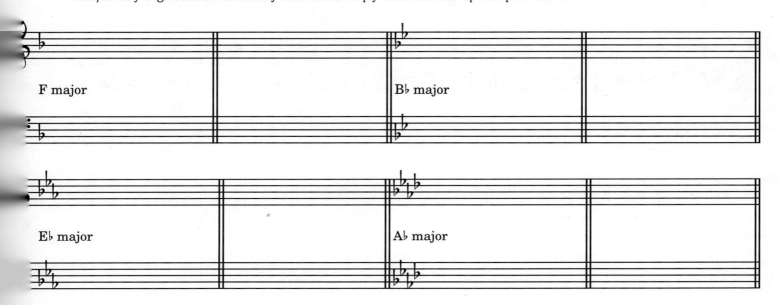

F major

B♭ major

E♭ major

A♭ major

HARMONIZING

1. Play through Roman numeral chords in closest position before harmonizing. If it helps you think of the chord pitches, pencil in the letter name next to the Roman numeral.

FRANZ JOSEPH HAYDN
(1732–1809)

2. Play also in D major and G major.

Americar

3. Use closest position. Add the slash (/) indications. The first one is done for you.

Germa

4. The first note of each measure of the chorus is given. Determine the rest by ear and play as you sing.

Goodnight, Ladies

American

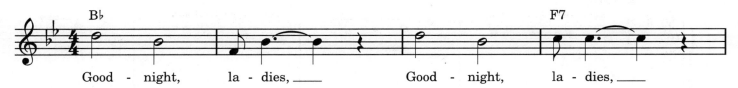

Good - night, la - dies, _____ Good - night, la - dies, _____

Good - night, la - dies, _____ We're going to leave you now.

Mer-ri-ly we roll a-long, Roll a-long, roll a-long. Mer-ri-ly we roll a-long, O'er the deep blue sea.

READING

1. With hand away from keyboard, think:

- Interval
- Keyboard location
- Fingering

Then play.

Play again, this time with the CD or MIDI disk background.

2

2. Use "tabletop" practice to secure finger crossings in measures 13 to 16, then play as written.

Hopak

ALEXANDER GOEDICKE
(1877–1957)

simile means to continue in a similar manner.

3. Count two measures of pulses before playing each example with an upbeat.

a.

1 2 3 | 1 2

b.

1 & 2 & | 1 & 2

c.

IMPROVISING

4-3

1. Create a blues trio in F:

- Part 1—melody based on the F blues pentascale

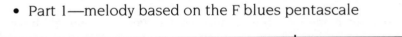

- Part 2—blues intervals that follow the I–IV–V pattern

      I   IV   V

- Part 3—walking bass that follows the I–IV–V pattern

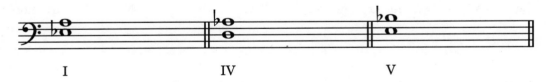

     I   IV   V

I	IV	I	I
IV	IV	I	I
V	IV	I	I

The CD or MIDI disk will provide a rhythm background. Play twice.

2. Improvise a right-hand melody to the rhythm of *Hey, Ho!* (p. 240). Use the following right-hand position. Then accompany with the ostinato shown.

RH Position

Ostinato

Now here is one traditional melody for *Hey, Ho!* Create your own left-hand ostinato using a low E and B.

Hey, Ho!

Englis

Hey, ho! No - bo - dy home. Meat nor drink nor mon-ey have I none,

Yet I will be mer - ry, mer - ry, mer - ry. Hey, ho! No - bo - dy home.

Next, establish a low ostinato for two people to play. Divide the balance of the group into four parts and perform as a round with ostinato. For part 1, play where written; for other parts, select different keyboard ranges.

PERFORMANCE

1. *Hello, Ma Baby* may be performed in several different ways. Try the following combinations according to the needs of your class:

- As a six-part ensemble, each student playing only one part.
- As a four-part ensemble, parts 2 and 3 combining into the Primo part and parts 4 and 5 into the Secondo part; parts 1 and 6 will remain single-line parts.
- As a duet, Primo and Secondo; parts 1 and 6 will be omitted.
- A combination of two options with the change occurring at the repeat.

Hello, Ma Baby

JOSEPH E. HOWARD
Arranged by Ann Collins

2.

Slow Bassin' Blues

MARTHA HILLEY

legato left hand throughout

*Crush note—play both notes at the same time and release the small note only!

3.

America the Beautiful

SAMUEL A. WARD
Arranged by Lynn Freeman Olson

4.

A Scalar Etude

MARTHA HILLEY

Not rushed

5.

Mellow Cello

LEE EVAN

15.

Compound Meter/Key Triads

LISTENING

15-1

1. You will hear a musical example with six sections, each one announced with a number. Only three different musical ideas are used. The first section can be labeled A. If the second section sounds the same, it will also be labeled A; if different, it will be called B. Somewhere, a C will also occur. The resulting order of letters is an outline of the *form*. Listen once, straight through. Then listen again, this time listing letters for the six sections.

    1. _____   4. _____

    2. _____   5. _____

    3. _____   6. _____

2. Locate the indicated keyboard position. Your teacher will play two-measure phrases and one final four-measure phrase. After your teacher has played the first phrase, repeat vocally. Your teacher will play the first phrase once again; now play this phrase on the keyboard. The same procedure will follow throughout the piece. Close your book!

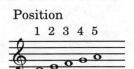

Position
1 2 3 4 5

Ear Investment No. 3

WOODY BUDNICK

3. You will hear three rhythm examples on the CD or MIDI disk. Tap back after each example.

5-2

RHYTHM

1. In each of the rhythms below, the eighth note receives one pulse. Count aloud as you tap the rhythms for each.

a.

> **Compound Meter** Time signature having a triple pulse within each basic beat:
>
> $\frac{6}{8}$ $\frac{9}{8}$ $\frac{12}{8}$

b.

c.

d.

e.

f.

g.

h.

i.

2. Tap and chant the following "spoken ensemble."

Song of the Pop-Bottler

Poem by MORRIS BISHOP

Arranged by Lynn Freeman Olson

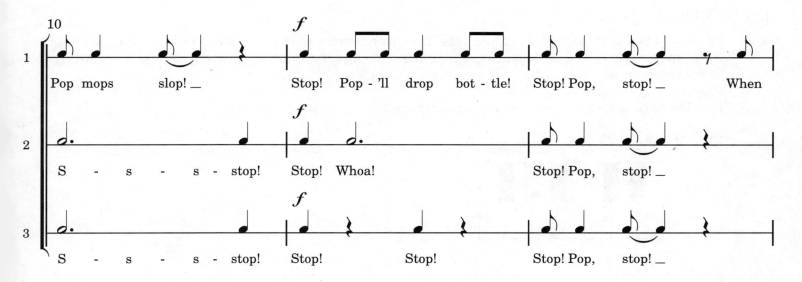

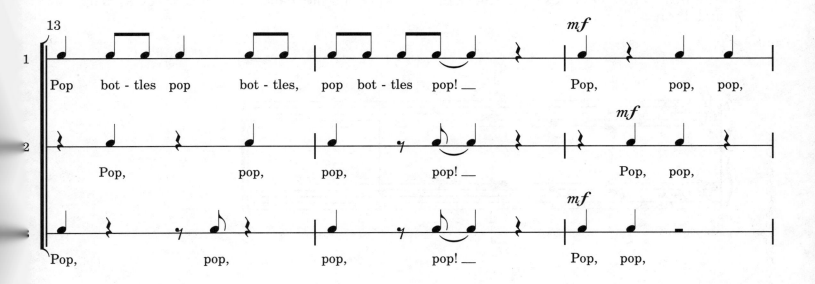

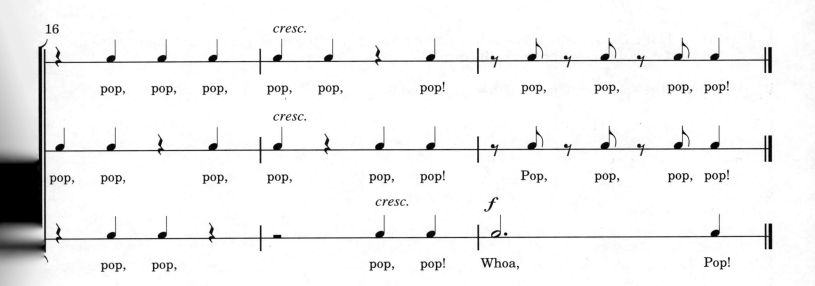

TECHNIQUE

The key of D-flat major contains five flats. The arrangement of the flats within the actual scale makes D-flat major one of the easiest scales to perform. To understand the grouping of fingerings, study the following example.

Play the two- and three-black-key groups, hands together, blocked.

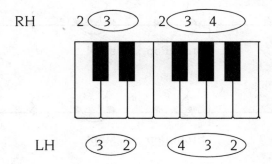

Play again, and this time use thumbs as pivots to move from one black-key group to the other (thumbs on F and thumbs on C). Block the D-flat major scale, hands together, two octaves up and down.

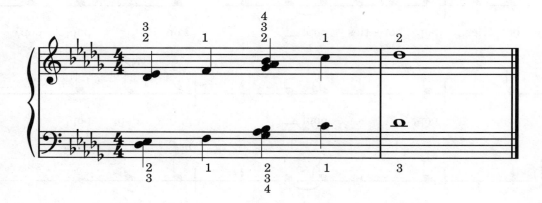

Now play the D-flat major scale as individual tones, hands together. Keep your fingers close to the keys, covering positions as shifts occur.

Transfer the same principle to G-flat major and B major.

THEORY

1. Play triads in the left hand on each tone of the C major scale. Determine the quality of each triad (major, minor, diminished).

Play triads in the left hand built on each tone of the following major scales:

    D   E   F   G   A

Play triads in the right hand built on each tone of the following major scales:

    D   E   F   G   A

15-3   Play triads, hands together, as directed by the CD or MIDI disk.

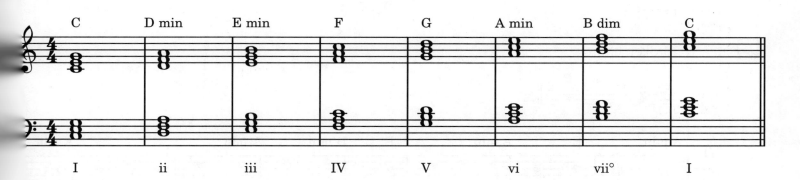

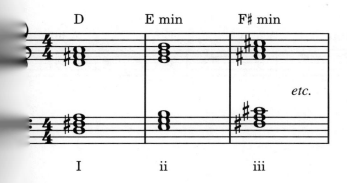

> **Relative Minor**   Shares the key signature of the relative major

2. All minor scales are derived from their relative majors and use the same key signatures. The *natural minor* scale can be observed within the major scale pattern, beginning on the sixth scale degree.

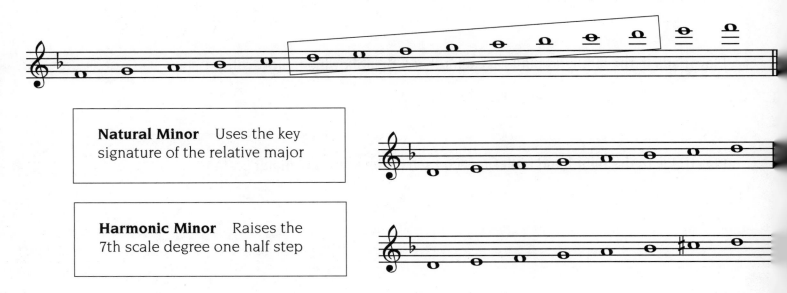

Natural Minor Uses the key signature of the relative major

Harmonic Minor Raises the 7th scale degree one half step

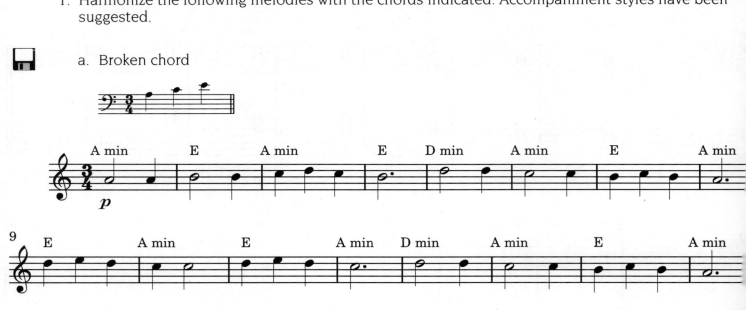

HARMONIZING

1. Harmonize the following melodies with the chords indicated. Accompaniment styles have been suggested.

a. Broken chord

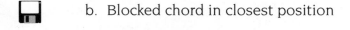

b. Blocked chord in closest position

c. Broken chord (two handed), play no melody!

Sometimes I Feel Like a Motherless Child

Spiritual

d. Root chord, fifth chord, as you sing!(two handed)

Red River Valley

American

e. Blocked chords

Allegro

I   V6   V$^6_4$ I6

I6   IV   I6   V$^6_4$ I6   I

f. Two-handed "boom-chick-chick" as your teacher plays melody

Andante

B♭   G min   E♭   F

B♭   E♭   F   B♭   E♭   B♭

g. Broken chord

Moderato

D min   A   D min   A   D min

G min   D min   A   D min   A

D min   A   D min   A   D min

READING

1. Play these examples that use minor keys.

a.

b.

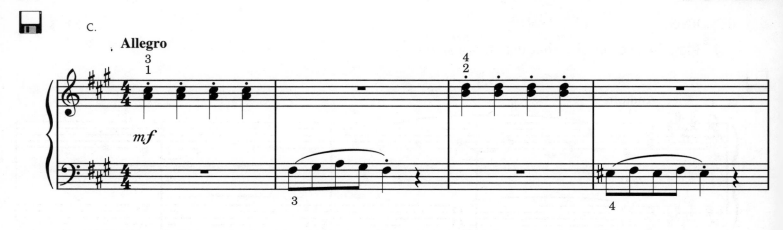

c.

Allegro

d.

Andante

RH

2. In what key is *Russian Song* written?

Russian Song

Russian
Arranged by Lynn Freeman Olson

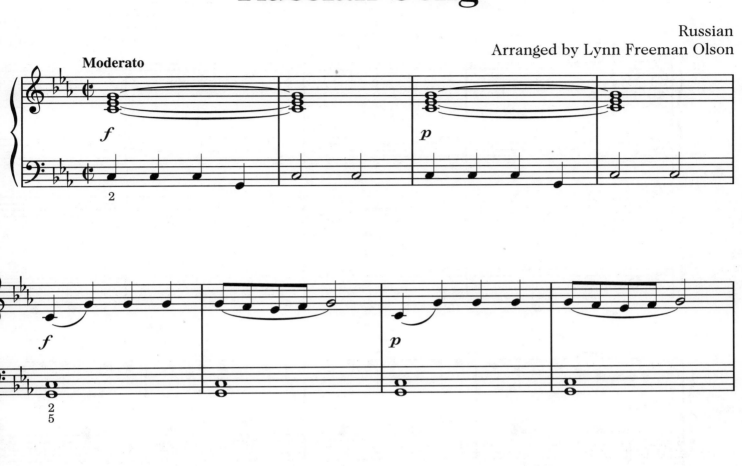

Joshua Fought the Battle of Jericho

Spiritu
Arranged by Martha Hill

IMPROVISING

Play *Country Dance* six times, moving to the next part down each time (part 6 moves to part 1). Part 3 should consist of chord tones *only*.

- First time, *p*
- Second time, *mp*
- Third time, *mf*
- Fourth time, *f*
- Fifth time, *p*
- Sixth time, *pp*

Country Dance

LYNN FREEMAN OLSON

PERFORMANCE

1.

Etude in D Minor

(original in A minor)

LOUIS KÖHLER
(1820–1886)

15

2.

All the Pretty Little Horses

Hush a bye, don't you cry, oh you pretty little baby.
When you wake, you'll have cake,
And all the pretty little horses.
A brown and gray, a black and bay,
And all the pretty little horses.

Traditional

Arranged by Tony Caramia

Festive Dance

CAROLYN MILLER

*Coda means "a tail."

Capelinha de Melão
(Little Chapel)
Secondo

Brazilian
Arranged by Rafael C. dos Santos

Capelinha de Melão
(Little Chapel)
Primo

Brazilian
Arranged by Rafael C. dos Santos

16.

Recap

PERFORMANCE
1.

Night Flight

LYNN FREEMAN OLSON

2.

Black Is the Color

American
Arranged by Robert Vandall

3.

The Entertainer

SCOTT JOPLIN
Arranged by Mark Nevin

16

D. S. al fine To turn back and repeat
from the sign 𝄋

4.

Home on the Range

American
Arranged by Lynn Freeman Olson

5.

Give My Regards to Broadway

GEORGE M. COHAN
(1878–1942)
Arranged by Lynn Freeman Olson

6.

Variations on a Theme by Haydn

JOHANNES BRAHMS
(1833–1897)
Arranged by Martha Hilley

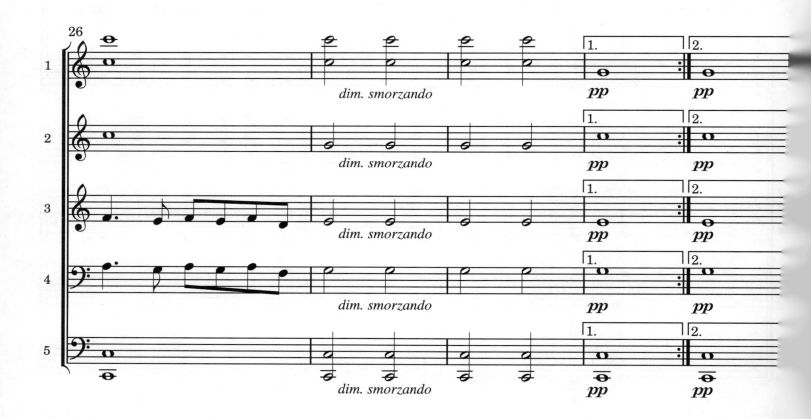

Smorzando	To die away

7.

Gypsy Dance

FRANZ JOSEPH HAYDN
(1732–1809)

TERMINOLOGY REVIEW

Discuss the following musical terms.

- *Accelerando/a tempo*
- Compound meter
- Inversion
- Major, minor, diminished, and augmented triads
- Relative minor
- Natural minor/harmonic minor
- Dominant seventh/C7/V7
- D. S. al fine
- Smorzando
- Coda

WRITING REVIEW

1. Indicate the inversion for each of the following chords by using the appropriate guitar symbol.

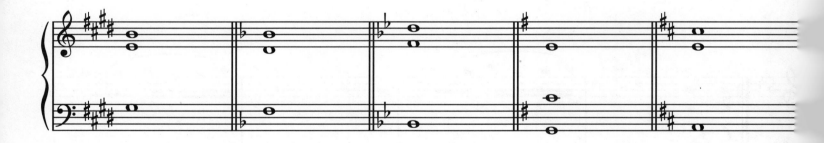

17.

Triplets/Primary Chords in Minor

LISTENING

1. Listen as your teacher plays the first phrase of the melody *Happy Birthday to You* in F major. The melody begins on the fifth scale tone. What is the meter?

   Listen again and play the phrase. Continue through the song.

2. Decide on another well-known melody or two you would like to play by ear. Proceed as in item 1 with your teacher's help as necessary.

3. Find the first three notes of the C minor scale; start on middle C. Your teacher will play two-measure phrases using these notes. Listen carefully for syncopation. Play back after each two-measure phrase. Close your book!

Ear Investment No. 4

WOODY BUDNICK

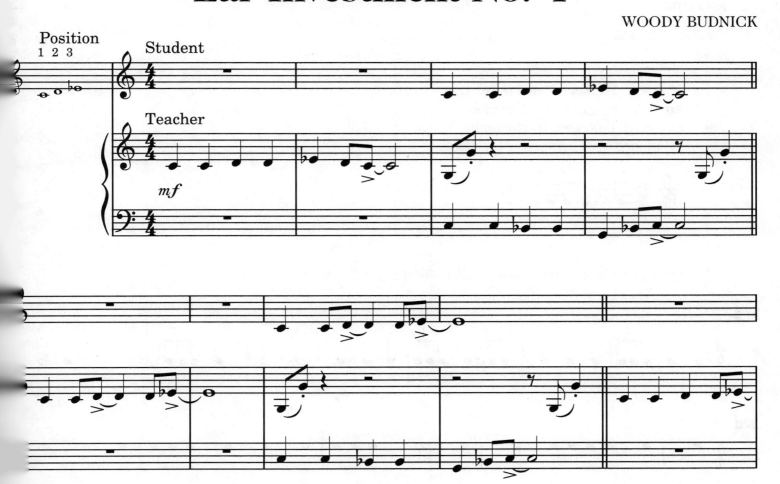

10

16

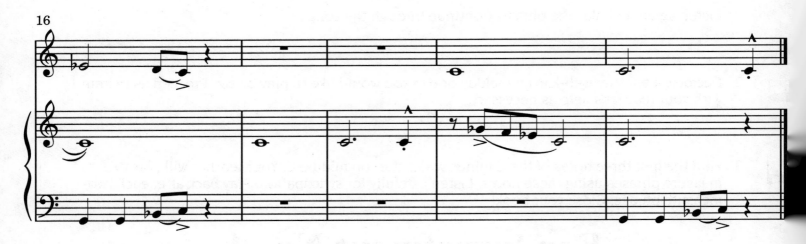

RHYTHM

Triplet Three notes that
are to be performed in the space
of a beat. Indicated by the figure
"3" placed above or below the notes.

1. Tap the following rhythm exercises containing triplets. Count aloud!

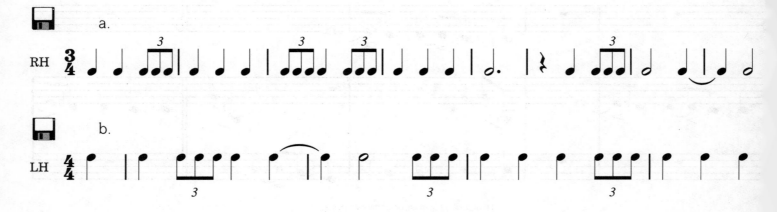

a.

b.

2. Tap the following two-handed rhythms that use triplets.

a.

b.

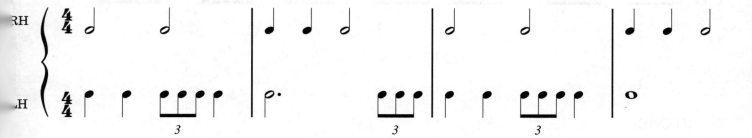

c.

3. Tap the following two-hand rhythm exercises that use compound rhythm.

a.

b.

TECHNIQUE

Study the pattern of fingering for the white-key minor scales, two octaves.

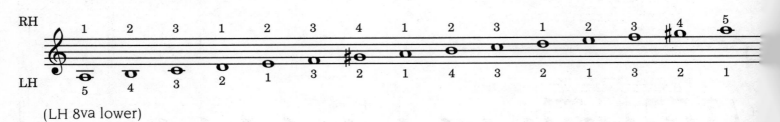

(LH 8va lower)

Does it look familiar?

Use this fingering in playing the following minor scales (natural and harmonic form), hands separately.

C   G   D   A   E

THEORY

1. Study the i, iv, and V chords as they are formed above the harmonic-minor scale. (Lowercase roman numerals are used for minor chords.)

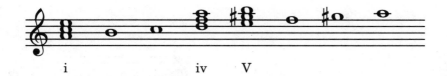

i   iv   V

Play the following exercises using i, iv, and V triads in harmonic minor. Spell the next triad aloud during each measure of rest.

a.

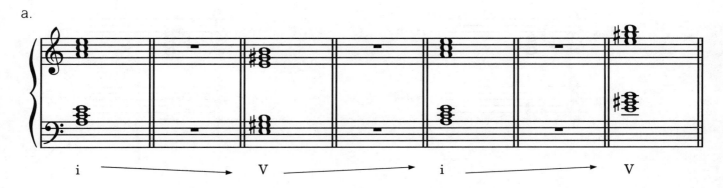

i   →   V   →   i   →   V

b.

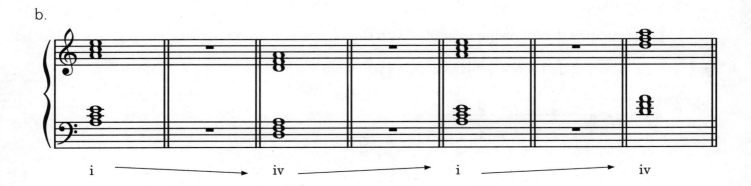

i   →   iv   →   i   →   iv

c.

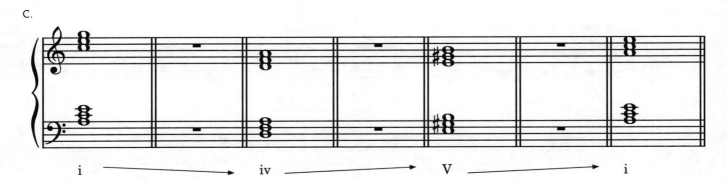

i   →   iv   →   V   →   i

Play the exercises again using these minor keys: C D E G.

2. There are many variations of writing guitar symbols for triads and seventh chords. The following table may help you to make up an accompaniment for a popular tune using the symbols shown in the particular piece of sheet music. The ability to figure out any chord lies in your ability to analyze the pattern of major and minor thirds used in the chord. Try playing these chords on other pitches and then "go for it"!

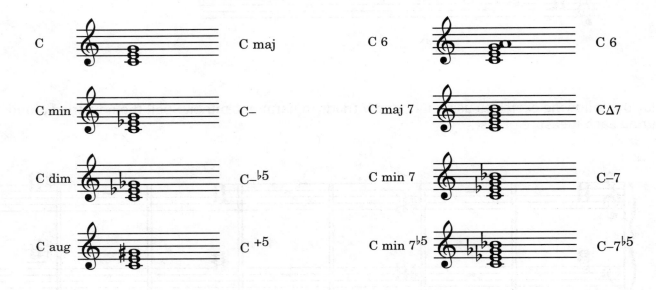

HARMONIZING

1. Harmonize the following melodies with the chords and accompanying suggestions indicated.

 a. Two-handed "boom-chick-chick" as you sing

Clementine

Americ

b. Broken chord or strumming pattern as you sing.

or

Scarborough Fair

British

Keyboard Style A style of accompanying in which the melody and chords are in the right hand (three notes); root or indicated bass note in the left hand.

The melody note must stay in the highest sounding voice in the right hand.

c. Keyboard style

Amazing Grace

American

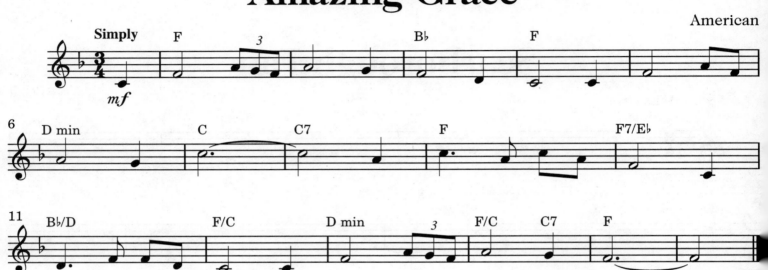

d. Blocked chords

Canterbury

Britis

e. Two-handed broken chord as you sing.

Lonesome Road

American

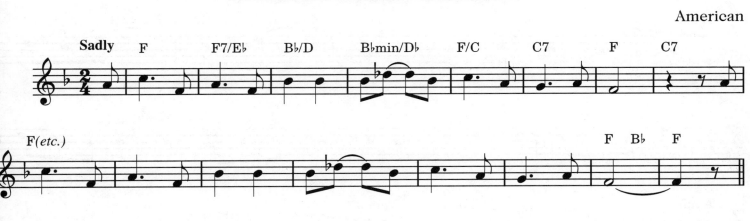

f. Complete in the style indicated.

Hush, Little Baby

American

2. Determine an appropriate accompaniment style and perform each of the three harmonizations.

When Johnny Comes Marching Home

American

3.

He's Got the Whole World

Spiritu

4.

Auld Lang Syne

Scottish

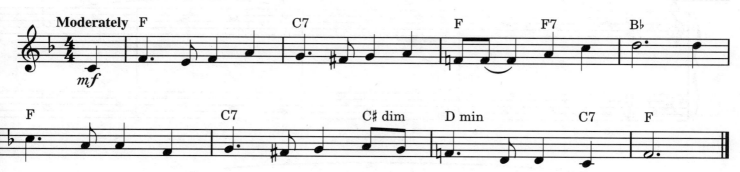

READING

1.

Streets of Laredo

American
Arranged by Lynn Freeman Olson

2.

Minuet in B Flat

LYNN FREEMAN OLSON

3.

Sadness

DANIEL GOTTLOB TÜRK
(1756–1813)

IMPROVISING

17-1

1. The melodic material found in most blues is based on the lyric, or the "sad tale of woe." Look closely at the verse written below and notice the repetition of the first and second set of four bars. The formula could be:

> State a problem (4 bars)
> Restate a problem (4 bars)
> Try to find a solution (4 bars)

Write two twelve-bar verses of your own to follow the verse shown. Improvise melodically as the CD or MIDI disk provides a background for three choruses of blues.

> I hate to see,
> That evenin' sun go down.
>
> Oh, I hate to see,
> That evenin' sun go down.
>
> That man of mine,
> He done left this town.

(The balance of this page has been left blank to eliminate a difficult page turn.)

316

PERFORMANCE

1.

The Frog Level Concerto*

JOSEPH M. MARTIN

*Frog Level is a small town in North Carolina.

17

2.

Two + Twelve

MARTHA HILLE

*If pedal is used, it must change with each ♩., except in final bar.

let it ring . . .

Rhythm Machine

LYNN FREEMAN OLSON

4.

Für Elise

(Albumblatt)

LUDWIG VAN BEETHOVEN
Arranged by William Gillock

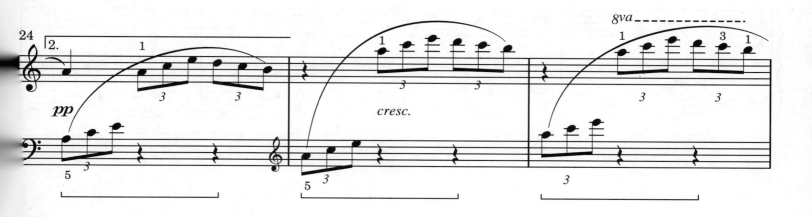

17

18.

18
Holiday Repertoire

1.

Shalom Chavarim

Arranged by Caroline Baxter

2.

It Came Upon the Midnight Clear

Edmund H. Sears

RICHARD S. WILLIS
Arranged by Lynn Freeman Olson

on the earth,_ good will to men, From heav-en's all - gra - cious King":_ The

world in sol - emn still - ness lay To hear the an - gels sing._

3.

I Saw Three Ships

I saw three ships come sailing in,
On Christmas day, on Christmas day,
I saw three ships come sailing in,
On Christmas day in the morning.

Traditional

Traditional
Arranged by Glenda Austin

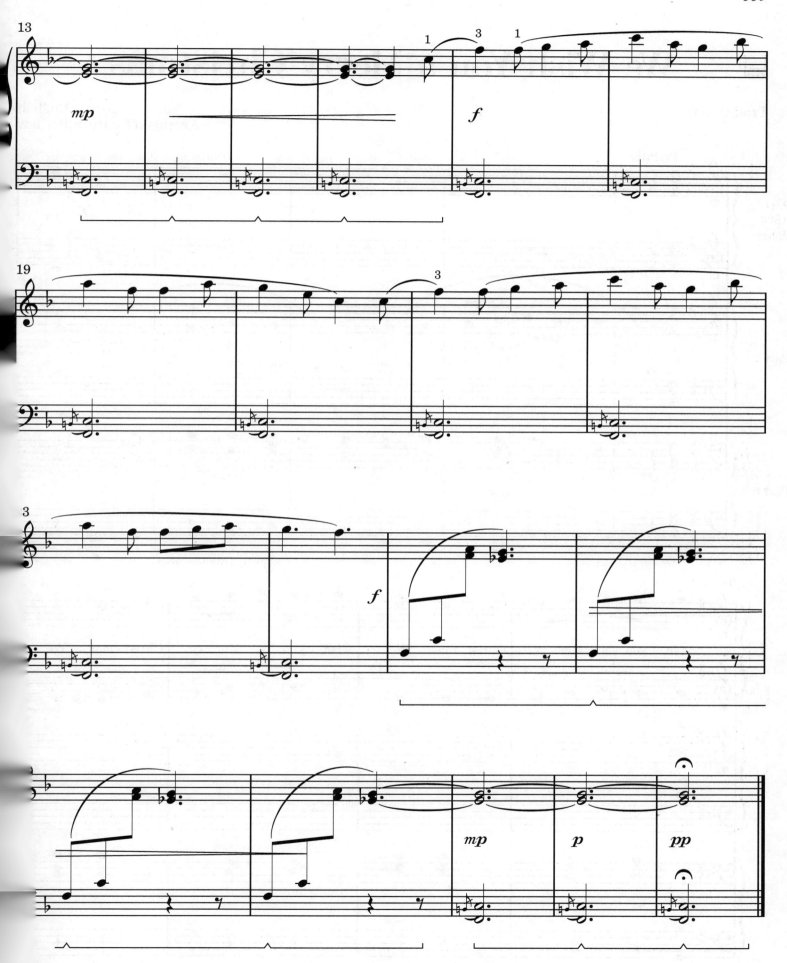

4.

We Wish You a Merry Christmas

Traditional

English
Arranged by Ruth Perdew

7.

Jingle Bell Jazz

Arranged by Susan Ogilvy

8.

Joy to the World

GEORGE FRIDERIC HANDEL
Arranged by Lynn Freeman Olson

9.

Hark! The Herald Angels Sing

FELIX MENDELSSOHN
(1809–1847)
Arranged by Martha Hilley

10.

O Christmas Tree

German
Arranged by Arletta O'Hearn

19.

19 Supplementary Repertoire

Etude in A Minor

GIUSEPPE CONCONE
(1801–1861)

2. Practice rhythms

Satin Latin

BILL BOYD

352

2.

Largo

SECONDO

G. F. HANDEL
Arranged by Chester Wallis

SECONDO

Largo

PRIMO

G. F. HANDEL
Arranged by Chester Wallis

PRIMO

4.

Musette

from J. S. Bach's *Notebook for Anna Magdalena Bach* (1725)

UNKNOWN

19

5.

German Dance

LUDWIG van BEETHOVEN, WoO 42
(1770–1827)

6.

Spinning Song
(Opus 14, No. 4)

ALBERT ELLMENREICH, Opus 14, No. 4

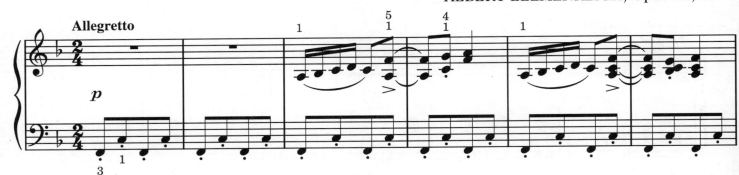

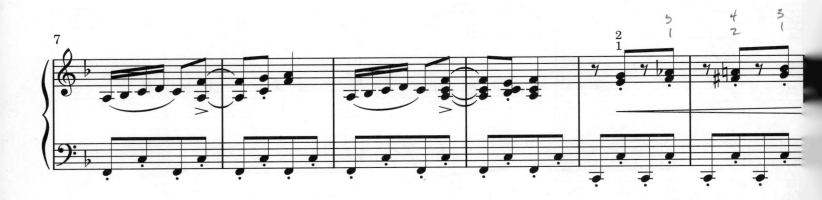

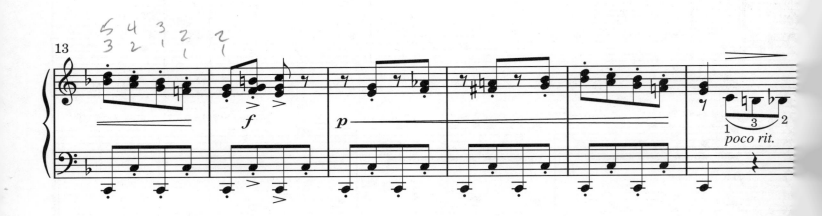

*Many students have found measures 27 to 42 more manageable if the hands are crossed: left hand *over* right hand plays the harmonic intervals while right hand plays the bass clef melody. If you have no technical difficulty as it is written and are able to maintain the opening tempo, disregard this suggestion.

360

The Swan

CAMILLE SAINT-SAËNS
Arranged by Betty Colley

8.

Moonlight

Up-stems RH
Down-stems LH

WILLIAM L. GILLOCK

Andante sostenuto (sustained)

9.

Prelude

SAMUIL MAYKAPAR
(1867–1938)

10.

Minuet

FRANZ JOSEPH HAYDN
(1732–1809)

11.

A Little Song

DIMITRI KABALEVSKY
(1904–1987)

12.

Prelude in C Major

from *The Well-Tempered Clavier*, Book I

JOHANN SEBASTIAN BACH
(1685–1750)

Appendix A — Major Keys

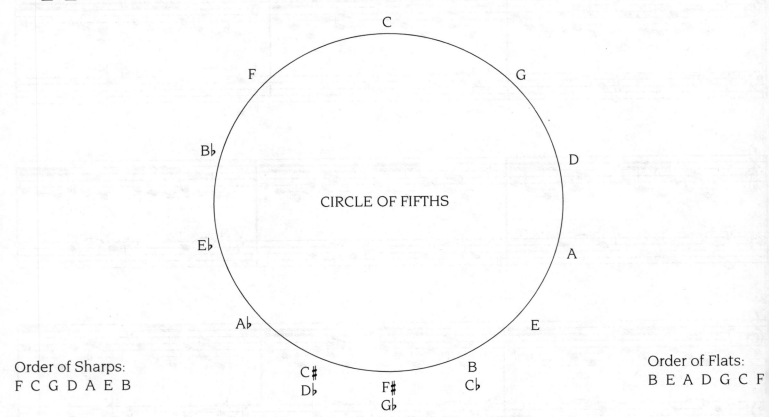

CIRCLE OF FIFTHS

Order of Sharps:
F C G D A E B

Order of Flats:
B E A D G C F

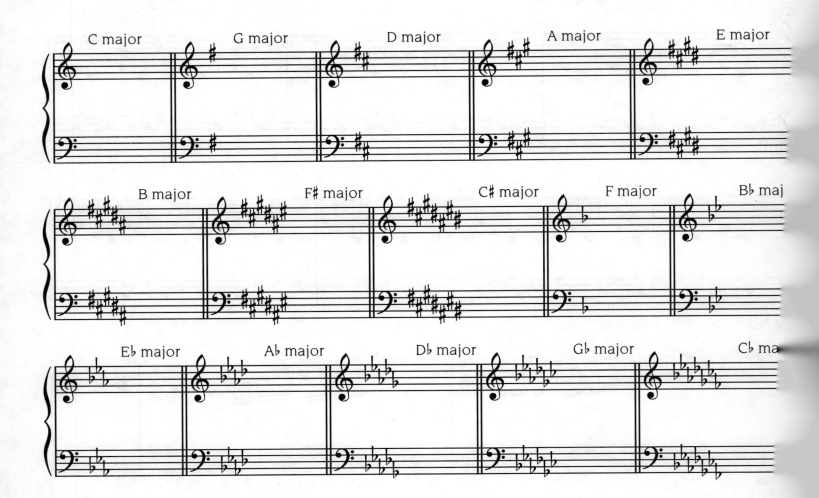

Appendix B — Major Scales

The following major scales use "black-key-group" fingering.

D-flat major

G-flat major

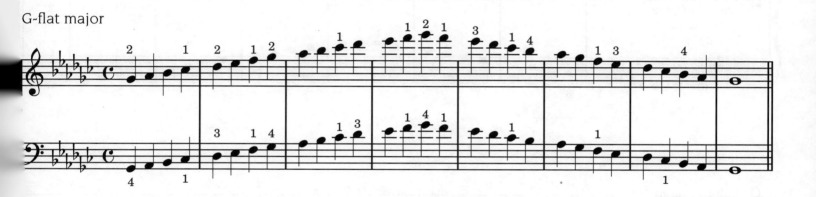

C-flat major

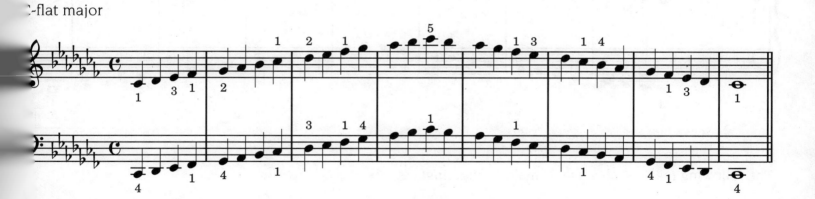

The following enharmonic scales use the same fingerings as above.

C-sharp major

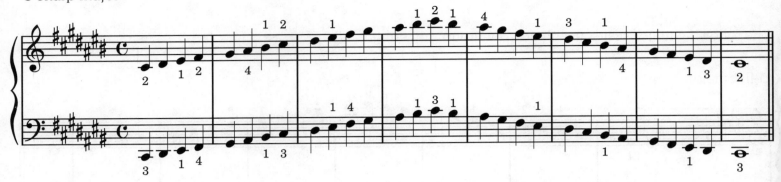

F-sharp major

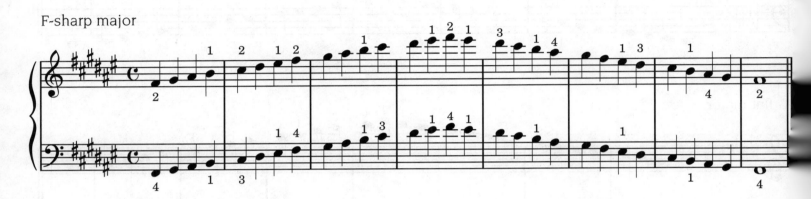

B major

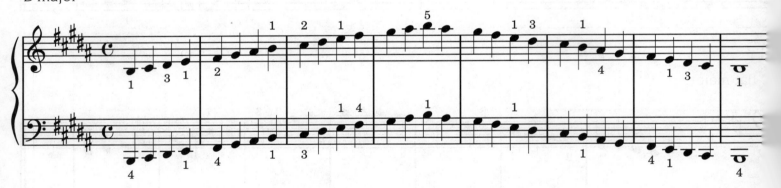

The following major scales use "C major" fingering.

C major

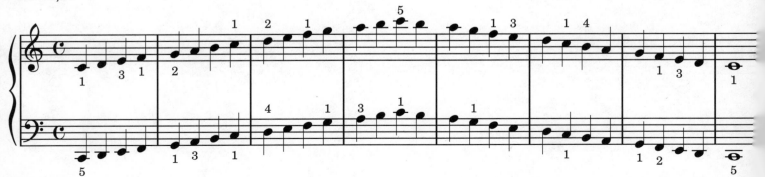

D major

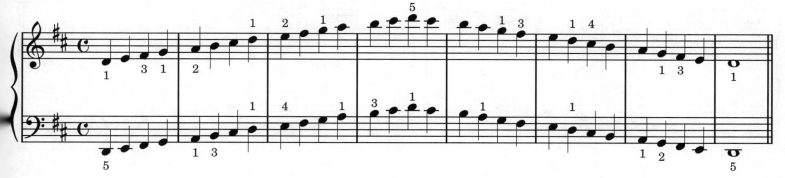

E major

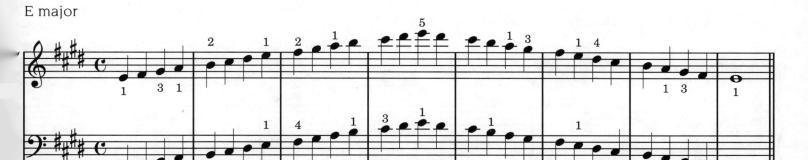

G major

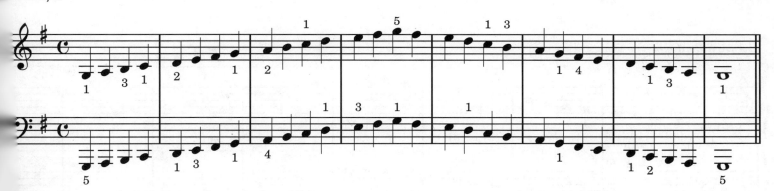

major

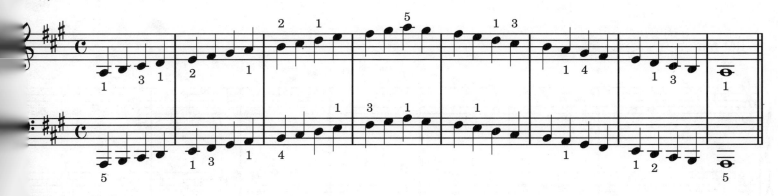

A-flat major (uses same fingering "combination" as C major)

The following major scales are often called "the other majors"!

F major

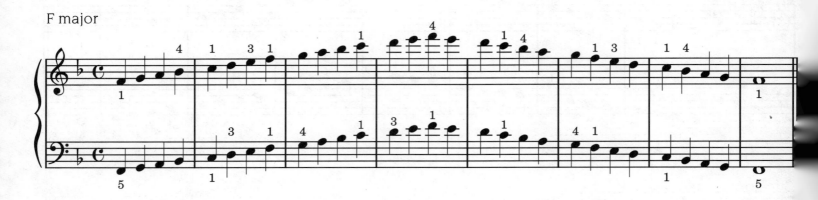

B-flat major

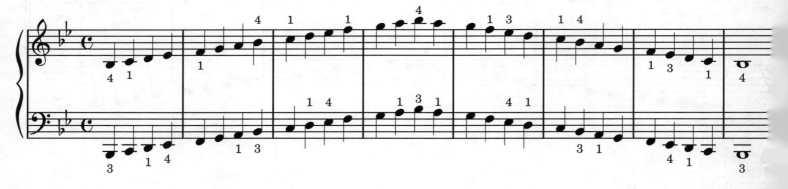

E-flat major

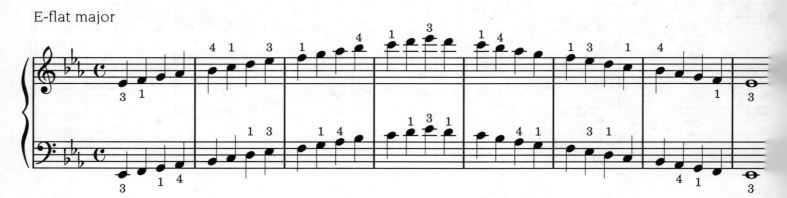

Appendix C — Minor Scales

These "harmonic" minor scales use C major fingering *or* the same fingering combinations as C major.

C minor

D minor

minor

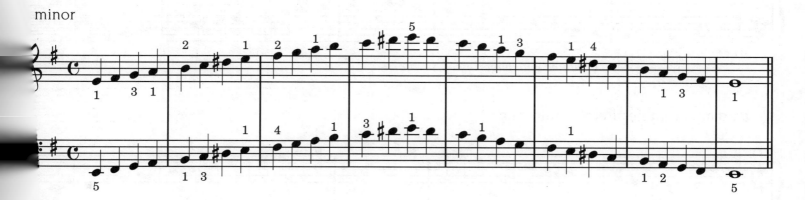

minor

A minor

A-flat minor

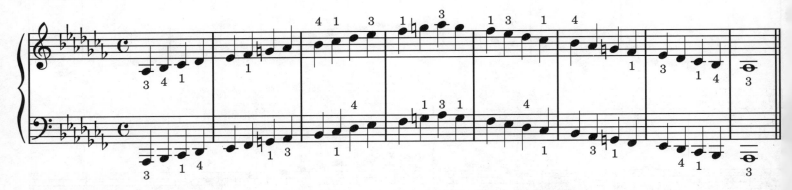

F-sharp minor (note alternate fingering)

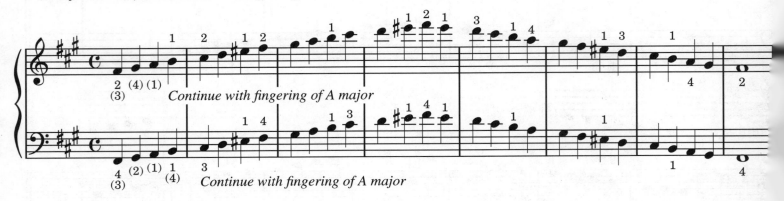

C-sharp minor (note alternate fingering)

The black-key-group minors use the same fingering combinations as the black-key-group majors.

B-flat minor

E-flat minor

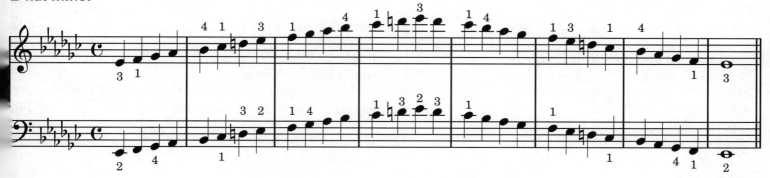

G-sharp minor

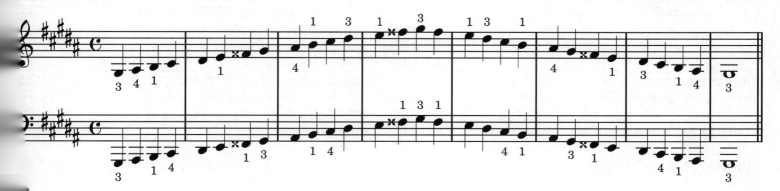

e the same fingering as F major!

inor

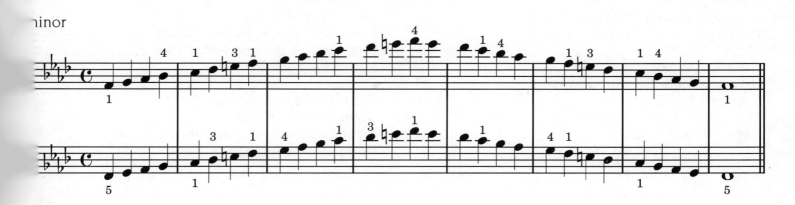

Index of Titles

Index of Composers